40 Irrefutable Signs of the Last Generation

40 IRREFUTABLE SIGNS OF THE LAST GENERATION
© 2010, Noah W. Hutchings

Printed in the United States of America

ISBN 1-933641-38-X

40 Irrefutable Signs of the Last Generation

Noah W. Hutchings

About the Author

Noah W. Hutchings was born in Choctaw County, Oklahoma, on December 11, 1922. He grew up in poverty during the days of the Great Depression, and worked for the National Recovery farm program of the Franklin Roosevelt Administration in the late '30s. In World War II he served three years in the South Pacific, first as a radar operator for a 90 mm antiaircraft battalion, and the last half of the war directed field artillery for the First Calvary Armored Division. After WWII he earned a university degree in Business Law and Management and took a part–time job as an accountant with Southwest Radio Church . . . and never left. At the ministry he increasingly took part in Gospel broadcasting and writing. He is given credit for writing 100 or more books and taken part in over 20,000 radio and television programs. He has led 53 Bible tours to Israel and many more to other parts of the world. He has actively led and participated in missions to Russia, China, Mongolia, Cuba, and other regions. At 87 he still works ten hours a day, travels abroad, and is actively involved in foreign missions.

A Partial Listing of other Books and Productions by Noah Hutchings

Commentaries
Daniel the Prophet
Revelation for Today
Jude: The Whole Realm of Rebellion

Other Books
Why So Many Churches?
Rapture and Resurrection
God: The Master Mathematician
God Divided the Nations
U.S. in Prophecy (with S. Frank Logsdon)
Petra in History and Prophecy

25 Messianic Signs in Israel Today
The New Creators
The Dark Side of the Purpose Driven Church
Which Bible Is God's Word? (with Gail Riplinger)

DVDs—filmed on site (1 hour each)
Touring Israel with Brother Hutchings
25 Messianic Signs in Israel Today
Petra in History and Prophecy

*Other titles are either out of print
or are of limited stock.*

**For additional information concerning prices and
the ministry of Southwest Radio Church of the Air, Inc.,
please call 1-800-652-1144,
or write to P.O. Box 100, Bethany, OK 73008.**

Please visit our website: www.swrc.com

Contents

Part I
Irrefutable Signs of the Last Days in the Secular World

Part I
Irrefutable Signs of the Last Days in the Secular World

After fifty–nine–plus years in the ministry, and according to some, having written more than one hundred books, I am still confused as to whether beginning remarks should be called a preface, introduction, foreword, or whatever. Nevertheless, not knowing the difference presents no handicap in advising the reader just why I wrote this book and why I think it is a good idea that he or she read it.

Regardless what the no–mils, mid–mils, all–mils, or gristmills say, there will be an END to this present world system, known in Scripture as the Church Age or the times of the gentiles. When the disciples asked Jesus, "What will be the sign of thy coming, and of the end of the world?" He didn't say, "Now, you boys have been reading too much scare gossip from those radical prophets, Isaiah, Ezekiel, Daniel, and Jeremiah."

No, indeed! Jesus carefully explained what the world would be like in the international, spiritual, moral, ecclesiastical, political, economic, and even heavenly spheres. Consider the Olivet Discourse in Matthew 24, Luke 21, and all the multitude of scriptures from almost every book in the Bible concerning the end of the age and the end of the world, there is no reason why any Christian, or church member, should be ignorant of the time on God's prophetic clock today except perhaps they have an ignorant pastor who either doesn't know or doesn't care.

This does not mean that we are to know the exact calendar date of Christ's return. In all examination of the prophetic scriptures relating to our day we must be credible. In 1988, the year I had a possible terminal illness with many more problems to deal with, one of our trustees had underwritten Edgar Whisenant in the writing and disseminating of his book *88 Reasons Why Jesus Will Return in 1988.* This trustee asked me three times to have the author on the broadcast and distribute his book.

Three times I refused, and this caused me additional problems. Had I done so, it would probably have meant the end of my ministry as well as the ministry of Southwest Radio Church. If Jesus had wanted us to know the exact date, He would have told us. But He did tell us the way the world would be when He would return.

Yet, I still continually get DVDs, CDs, and books with hours or hundreds of pages calculating the exact day Jesus would return, and even the time of that day. After listening to hours of these recordings, watching the visuals, or reading the books, the answer may be in the last minute or last page why He will return in A.D. 2113 at twelve noon is because there are 2,113 sentences in the Bible that do not end with a period. (Please don't try to count the scriptures in the Bible that do, or do not, end with a period.)

When I get such prophetic meanderings, I feel obligated to at least review them, but I usually end up as frustrated as trying to answer my wife's twentieth question about why I got a haircut before picking up a loaf of bread at the local market.

It is probable that no more than 5 percent of church members today ever heard a single reference by their pastor to the prophetic signs of our time. This is in spite of two world wars in the past century with multiple regional wars such as the Korean War, the Vietnam War, the Iraq War, etc., Israel refounded, space travel, nuclear weapons, modern inventions like the radio and television, and many, many other contemporary events prophesied in the Bible.

"Ho, hum," as Peter said they would say, ". . . there shall come in the last days scoffers, walking after their own lusts, And saying, Where is the promise of his coming? . . . all things continue as they were from the beginning . . ." (2 Peter 3:3–4). Jesus Himself warns from Heaven: "Behold, I come as a thief. Blessed is he that watcheth . . ." (Revelation 16:15).

The most serious message deficit in Christendom today, including the contemporary evangelical churches, is declaring the prophetic signs of our time in respect to the Second Coming of Jesus Christ. An awareness of the soon coming of Jesus Christ should be the most pressing motivation for Christians to win the lost while there is yet time, and this is the reason for this book.

Why 40 Prophetic Signs?

Forty is the biblical number of probationary judgment. Jonah's message to the Assyrians was that unless there was repentance in forty days, Nineveh would be destroyed. Israel was under the probationary judgment of God for forty years in the wilderness. Jesus was tempted of the devil for forty days. From Adam to Jesus Christ was exactly four thousand years. "But when the fulness of the time was come, God sent forth his Son . . ." (Galatians 4:4). The context of Paul's statement was that if God had not sent forth His son to redeem man from his sins, there would have been no reason to extend the time of the human race.

Peter and John preached to Israel that if the nation would repent of killing Jesus Christ, their rightful Messiah, and cry out to God to send Him back, the millennial kingdom would come in at that time (Acts 3:19–20). But less than 1 percent in Israel acknowledged Jesus Christ as Lord, so He did not come back. According to Jesus' promise in Matthew 23:39, He will not return to Israel until every Israelite will welcome Him as Savior, Lord, and King of Kings. Paul was on good prophetic ground when he said that in that day, all Israel would be saved.

However, because Israel under the influence of the Sadducees and Pharisees rejected the claims of Jesus Christ, the probationary judgment that He delivered on the Mount of Olives in Matthew 24 came to pass exactly forty years later in A.D. 70 when the Romans destroyed Jerusalem, the temple, and those that were not killed of the able–bodied were sold on the world slave markets.

The generation of Jesus' day in Israel was judged in A.D. 70, which could imply that a generation according to time would be seventy years. This would also coincide with the years of man in Psalm 90. The generation in Israel who were turned back from the Promised Land because of unbelief perished in the wilderness over a period of forty years, which could mean that a generation is forty years. I served in the Army during World War II, and I noted an article recently that my generation was now dying at the rate of one thousand a day. My understanding of the word "generation" is that it applies to people rather than a specific time period, meaning a certain race or of a certain nationality or religion that is associated with a certain event in history. Of course, any generation will pass from the world stage soon, depending upon world events or the natural course of age.

Nevertheless, the Bible references a particular generation to whom specific signs related to the Second Coming of Jesus Christ would be given: "Verily I say unto you, This generation shall not pass away, till all be fulfilled" (Luke 21:32). Preterists will contend Jesus here in this verse was speaking of the generation that lived in A.D. 70 when Jerusalem was destroyed, but this cannot be possible, because this same generation mentioned in Luke 21 would also ". . . see the Son of man coming in a cloud with power and great glory" (Luke 21:27). Certainly, the generation of A.D. 70 did not see the Second Coming of Jesus Christ.

It is also evident from the context of Matthew 24 and Luke 21 that the progressive fulfillment, or appearance of, signs of the end of the age would occur, or lead to, ". . . great tribulation, such as was not since the beginning of the world to this time, no, nor ever shall be" (Matthew 24:21).

Now, in this book, if I can prove to the agnostic world and the sleeping church members, including pastors, of the forty probationary signs in international affairs, wars, science, morality, ecclesiastics, economics, education, and other areas of national and international activities and thought, would it not be credible evidence that the coming of the Lord is near, "even at the doors" (Matthew 24:33)?

The odds that forty events or conditions, prophesied from two to five thousand years ago, would all come to pass in our present generation are almost beyond computation. God has given mankind today all this evidence so that he will be without excuse when the judgments of the Great Tribulation come.

It is the understanding of fundamental Bible scholars that all true Christians will be taken out of the world before this judgment comes (1 Thessalonians 4:13–18). Everyone is advised to "Watch ye therefore, and pray always, that ye may be accounted worthy to escape all these things that shall come to pass, and to stand before the Son of man" (Luke 21:36).

Therefore, some will escape as explained in 1 Thessalonians 4:13–18, and according to the promise to all who have received Jesus Christ as Savior and Lord, God promises, ". . . I also will keep thee from the hour of temptation, which shall come upon all the world, to try them that dwell upon the earth" (Revelation 3:10).

It has been my prayer that one day I could write a book so clearly setting forth the signs of Christ's coming applicable for our present time that no one could deny them. I pray that this book will be an answer to my prayer and that it lead many to be saved from the coming tribulation that will be on all the world.

SIGN NUMBER 1

INCREASE IN THE SPEED OF TRAVEL

In the first thirteen hundred years after the creation of the first man and woman, the human race increased to an estimated population of between 9 and 10 billion, according to Dr. Lambert Dolphin. This was because men and women, according to the Bible, lived to between eight and nine hundred years, and some even longer. It also appears evident that the world was greatly different at that time in terms of environment and food–producing plants and vegetables. We would also assume that early man migrated over the landmasses of the earth as they existed at that time. As proven by actual photographs reproduced in the book *Evolution and Human Fossil Footprints* by Dr. Aaron Judkins, man and dinosaurs existed together on every continent.

According to the Bible, a world flood destroyed the earth's first civilization of mankind with the exception of four men and four women. Over the next three or four hundred years mankind increased once more to a considerable number, but seemed content to remain in one area under the authority of one man, called Nimrod. Therefore, we read from the Bible, Genesis 11:8–9: "So the LORD scattered them abroad from thence upon the face of all the earth: and they left off to build the city. Therefore is the name of it called Babel; because the LORD did there confound the language of all the earth: and from thence did the LORD scatter them abroad upon the face of all the earth."

I understand that the so–called modern historical and scientific authority will not accept the biblical record as irrefutable evidence. However, it must be acknowledged that the Masoretic text of the Old Testament, as verified by Josephus and other notable historians, is one of the oldest preserved writings of an organized national society in the world. Hundreds of the places, people, and events recorded in the Old Testament have been verified by archaeology. I have personally been to hundreds of sites recorded in the Bible that existed three to four thousand years ago.

The biblical record relates that mankind was separated into nations after the seventy grandsons of the pre–flood patriarch Noah according to race, language, culture, talents, and natural affinities. They were also to be kept separated by oceans, continents, rivers, deserts, mountains, and distance. However, just as it is natural to be the leader of the pack, this motivation is also true collectively of tribes, races, or nations. This is why nations become empires—Egyptian Empire, Assyrian Empire, Babylonian Empire, Roman Empire, British Empire, etc. The Roman Empire in its subdivided status (British Empire, French Empire, German Empire, etc.) almost succeeded in once again uniting the entire human race under one political entity, but it never quite succeeded. While oceans, mountains, and deserts, plus natural racial differences were serious deterrents to the forming of another Babel, the real problem was distance.

Nevertheless, the Bible, and particularly the book of Daniel, prophesied of the future date in time when another Babel would be formed. The leader or team at this end–time world empire would be called the "man of sin," and the nations of the world would be at his "steps," figuratively meaning walking distance. Thus, the landmass of the world would have to be made smaller, or distances would have to be made less by traveling from point A to point B quicker.

Daniel prophesied of the time when another world empire would arise:

And at that time shall Michael stand up, the great prince which standeth for the children of thy people: and there shall be a time of trouble, such as never was since there was a nation even to that same time: and at that time thy people shall be delivered, every one that shall be found written in the book. And many of them that sleep in the dust of the earth shall awake, some to everlasting life, and some to shame and everlasting contempt. And they that be wise shall shine as the brightness of the firmament; and they that turn many to righteousness as the stars for ever and ever. But thou, O Daniel, shut up the words, and seal the book, **even to the time of the end: many shall run to and fro,** and knowledge shall be increased.

—Daniel 12:1–4

Adam could get on a horse and travel at a speed of perhaps twenty–five miles an hour, but he could probably go only a mile or two at that speed before the horse became tired. Man was confined to this rate of travel until 1679 (5,679 years later), when Thomas Savery of England, a military engineer, made the first steam engine. Although the Savery steam engine was used only to pump water out of mines, James Watts in 1769 improved Savery's engine and made it able to turn the wheels on a carriage. By 1820 the steam engine was adapted to turn propellers on ships, doubling or tripling their sailing speeds, and by 1850 steam engines were pushing trains across the United States at speeds of forty to fifty miles an hour. The world was becoming smaller.

From the first crude steam engines later came the gasoline engine and then the jet engine. Today, 6,010 AA (after Adam), I can get up at four a.m. and be in Moscow or Beijing by ten p.m. I have done so many times. The world has become many times smaller than it was when Julius Caesar crossed the Rubicon.

"... **Many shall run to and fro ...**": *Ward's Motor Vehicle Facts and Figures* reports that there were 685,954,000 cars registered worldwide, and 385,404,000 trucks and buses, for a total—worldwide—of 1,071,358,000 motor vehicles. The average miles driven per vehicle per year is 9,000. That comes to 9,642,222,000,000 miles per year.

According to CNN News, traffic jams in the United States cost Americans $68 billion each year in wasted time and fuel. The average rush–hour driver—not just commuters, but all drivers—wastes about sixty–two hours in traffic each year.

More than 1.6 billion people worldwide fly annually according to the International Air Transport Association. By the year 2010,

research suggests it will reach 2.3 billion. At the present time, more than 500,000 airline passengers cross international borders every day.

The staggering numbers of those who run to and fro on trains and subways are estimated to be 100 billion–plus each year. The New York City subway system *alone* has an annual ridership of 1.4 billion. Japan Railways operates 26,000 trains with more than a million riders *daily*.

The following is a list of the ten rail systems, underground subways, and metros in the world that receive the most passengers per year:

Moscow	3.2 billion
Tokyo	2.7 billion
Paris	2.26 billion
Mumbai	2.22 billion
Seoul	1.6 billion
New York City	1.4 billion
Mexico City	1.3 billion
Osaka	957 million
London	886 million
Hong Kong	798 million

Somebody is doing a lot of running to and fro!

Daniel prophesied that at the end of the age, just before God would fulfill His covenants with Israel and the Messiah would reign on this earth, ". . . many would run to and fro. . . ." The only deterrent to man running to and fro today seems to be the high price of gasoline, road construction, and red traffic lights.

Someone recently asked me how I could keep working at eighty–seven years of age. I replied that God has given us a seventy–year warranty, but that does not include the time we wait at red lights.

I thank God there are not going to be any red lights in Heaven. No flashing red police car lights, because there will be no criminals in Heaven. No flashing red lights on ambulances, because there will be no illness or pain in Heaven. And while I have no idea how much running to and fro we will be doing in Heaven, our Creator who made light to go at 186,000–plus miles per second can take care of any traffic problems without the aid of traffic lights.

Regardless, and without any credible contradiction, the appearance of trains, planes, and automobiles to make possible the increase of speed and travel, incredibly decreasing the size of the planet, is a major prophetic sign that the coming of the Lord Jesus Christ within this last generation is evident.

No one can credibly contradict this important sign that is being fulfilled in this last generation before the coming of our Lord Jesus Christ.

Sign Number 2

Increase of Knowledge

. . . and some to shame and everlasting contempt. And they that be wise shall shine as the brightness of the firmament; and they that turn many to righteousness as the stars for ever and ever. But thou, O Daniel, shut up the words, and seal the book, even to the time of the end: many shall run to and fro, **and knowledge shall be increased.**

—Daniel 12:2–4

It is said that 80 percent of the world's total knowledge has been brought forth in the last decade, and that 90 percent of all the scientists who have ever lived are alive today.

One Hundred Years Ago . . .

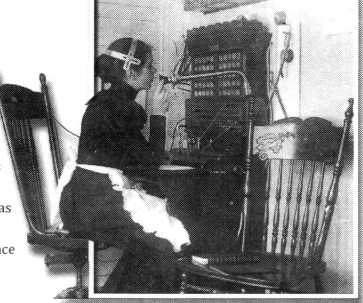

» The average life expectancy was 47 years old.
» Only 14 percent of homes had a bathtub.
» Only 8 percent of homes had a telephone.
» There were only 8,000 cars and 144 miles of paved roads.
» The maximum speed limit in most cities was 10 miles per hour.
» More than 95 percent of all births took place at home.
» The average wage was 22 cents an hour.

» Eggs were 14 cents a dozen.
» Coffee was 15 cents a pound.
» Most women only washed their hair once a month . . . with Borax or egg yolks for shampoo.
» The population of Las Vegas, Nevada, was 30.
» Canada passed a law prohibiting poor people from entering.

The Hebrew word for "increase" (*ra–ba–h*) implies not only an addition of knowledge, but also of multiplication or a knowledge that is increasing exponentially. This is an exact prophecy. Knowledge is now presently doubling every twenty–two months. We are living in the "Information Age," making this sign even more obvious.

What used to take an entire room . . .

Every *minute* they add *two hundred pages* to man's scientific knowledge, and the scientific material produced every *twenty–four hours* would take one person *five years* to read. About *half a million* new books are published every year.

When Apollo 13 was lost in space, computers worked out in an hour and a half a way to bring it back. It is reported that it would have taken a scientist working with pencil and paper over a million years to figure out how to perform the same feat.

In 1994, a computer chip could hold 3.1 million transistors, more than twice as many as the previous year's model. By the end of the decade, a chip will contain more information than a billion transistors.

Twentieth century technology has increased, not a little at a time, but exponentially. You can sit in the quiet of your own home and drown yourself in information from the Inter-

. . . is now smaller than a penny!!

net. We used to be in awe of how many volumes of information could fit on a computer CD disk, but now a DVD can hold up to four times as much information as a typical CD!

Tiny babies weighing less than one pound can survive outside the womb, and unborn babies can undergo surgery before birth. We can clone sheep, mice, and cattle. We have the technology to clone humans as well, and before too long, I'm sure someone will.

Since Eve ate the fruit of the forbidden "tree of knowledge," women have been generally deprived of access to higher education. With the prophesied increase of knowledge in the last generation, women from all over the world are now receiving doctorates, even some in the Muslim world. According to the National Opinion Research Center, women are now receiving an astounding 41.8 percent of the Ph.Ds granted. Those of both genders from African, Hispanic, and Asian descent receiving doctorates was 89.3 percent higher in 2008 than in 1988. This represents an accelerated exponential increase in knowledge in just the past few years (*Chicago Chronicle,* July 27, 2009).

The National Science Foundation reported that in 2007 that in just the U.S. alone, 48,079 Ph.Ds in science were granted by universities, and that increases in the number of Ph.Ds in physics and engineering were growing at more than 13 percent yearly (*Argosy University,* July 27, 2009).

As Daniel prophesied, in this last generation knowledge is exploding in both genders, in all races, in all nations as never before in man's history.

Man's knowledge today is manifested in the millions of university degree holders being turned out each year by the higher institutions of learning, but how many of them have the wisdom to use the knowledge they have earned? The wisdom of the ages is more than wearing socks darker than your pants. "The fear of the LORD is the beginning of wisdom: and the knowledge of the holy is understanding" (Proverbs 9:10).

The reality of God who created all things is disputed, not feared, in practically every institution of higher learning today. Education today is not for making man better or more holy, but rather for making him more evil and ungodly. Without knowledge of God, education only leads to self–destruction.

Man's history began by rejecting God for knowledge (Genesis 2), and it will end the same way (Revelation 22). Each tree bears its own fruit in due season, and the tree of knowledge is no exception.

It cannot be disputed that the exponential increase of knowledge is a sure sign of the last generation. The ultimate fruit of man's knowledge is the hundreds of H–bombs available today, enough to destroy this present generation many times over.

Now, we don't have to wonder why God did not want Adam and Eve to eat of the tree of knowledge. Knowledge in and of itself is good, just as rat poison is 99 percent good. It is unregenerate men who use it for evil instead of good. Thus, the more knowledge man has, the more evil the world becomes. Evolution is the most evil imagination or invention of Satan or man, yet it is the basis for all modern education.

Solomon determined to gain knowledge and wisdom, and he gained the reputation of being the wisest man in the world, yet we read in Ecclesiastes, "Then said I in my heart, As it happeneth to the fool, so it happeneth even to me; and why was I then more wise? Then I said in my heart, that this also is vanity" (Ecclesiastes 2:15). He ended up with seven hundred wives, three hundred concubines, and his nation had a huge debt and a heavy tax burden. Like Israel under Solomon, we have thousands of universities, millions graduating with Masters and Doctoral degrees, yet we also have the greatest sin problem, the highest taxes, and an impossible multitrillion-dollar debt.

In addition to all our schools and educational resources, there is the Internet. In a minute's time I have at my fingertips all the knowledge and information that has ever been gained or published on any subject, or any visible or invisible thing that exists, ever existed, or possibly ever will exist.

Daniel said that at the time of the end, knowledge would increase. This is another irrefutable truth that these are the last days of the last days.

Sign Number 3

End–Time Nations and Empires

The continuing apostasy that engulfed the northern kingdom of Israel ended in 700 B.C. when God allowed the Assyrian kingdom to invade the nation and take into captivity the ten tribes that had rebelled against the reign of Solomon's son, Jereboam. The southern kingdom, Judah, continued in periods of intermittent apostasy and revival until the Lord told Josiah that although he was a good king, he could not spare the nation any longer. Finally in about 600 B.C. God allowed Babylon to invade and conquer Judah. In 586 B.C., after the king of Babylon tired of trying to deal with a rebellious people, he ordered Jerusalem and the temple to be destroyed and the most educated and healthy citizens be brought to Babylon for use as slaves. Among those captives taken to Babylon was a young royal heir by the name of Daniel, who ended up in the king's court as one of his wise men, or counselors. In due course the king, Nebuchadnezzar, was worried about a dream that he had forgotten and demanded his wise men tell him not only the dream, but the interpretation of the dream. God gave Daniel both the dream and what it meant, as follows:

Thou, O king, sawest, and behold a great image. This great image, whose brightness was excellent, stood before thee; and the form thereof was terrible. This image's head was of fine gold, his breast and his arms of silver, his belly and his thighs of brass, His legs of iron, his feet part of iron and part of clay. Thou sawest till that a stone was cut out without hands, which smote the image upon his feet that were of iron and clay, and brake them to pieces. Then was the iron, the clay, the brass, the silver, and the gold, broken to pieces together, and became like the chaff of the summer threshingfloors; and the wind carried them away, that no place was found for them: and the stone that smote the image became a great mountain, and filled the whole earth. This is the dream; and we will tell the interpretation thereof before the king. Thou, O king, art a king of kings: for the God of heaven hath given thee a kingdom, power, and strength, and glory. And wheresoever the children of men dwell, the beasts of the field and the fowls of the heaven hath he given into thine hand, and hath made thee ruler over them all. Thou art this head of gold. And after thee shall arise another kingdom inferior to thee, and another third kingdom of brass, which shall bear rule over all the earth. And the fourth kingdom shall be strong as iron: forasmuch as iron breaketh in pieces and subdueth all things: and as iron that breaketh all these, shall it break in pieces and bruise. And whereas thou sawest the feet and toes, part of potters' clay, and part of iron, the kingdom shall be divided; but there shall be in it of the strength of the iron, forasmuch as thou sawest the iron mixed with miry clay. And as the toes of the

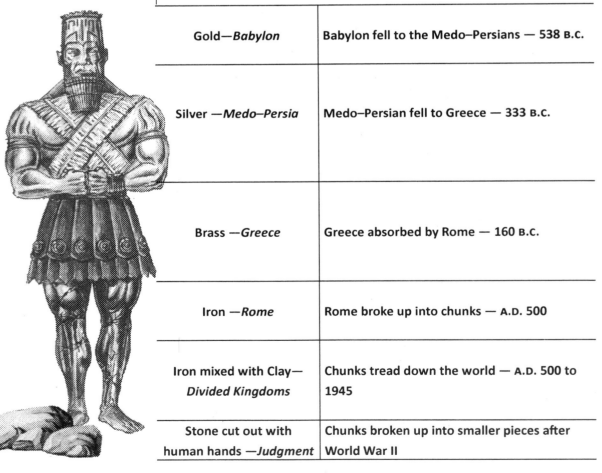

Gold—*Babylon*	**Babylon fell to the Medo–Persians — 538 B.C.**
Silver —*Medo–Persia*	**Medo–Persian fell to Greece — 333 B.C.**
Brass —*Greece*	**Greece absorbed by Rome — 160 B.C.**
Iron —*Rome*	**Rome broke up into chunks — A.D. 500**
Iron mixed with Clay— *Divided Kingdoms*	**Chunks tread down the world — A.D. 500 to 1945**
Stone cut out with human hands —*Judgment*	**Chunks broken up into smaller pieces after World War II**

Stone fills whole earth —*Christ's Kingdom*

feet were part of iron, and part of clay, so the kingdom shall be partly strong, and partly broken. And whereas thou sawest iron mixed with miry clay, they shall mingle themselves with the seed of men: but they shall not cleave one to another, even as iron is not mixed with clay. And in the days of these kings shall the God of heaven set up a kingdom, which shall never be destroyed: and the kingdom shall not be left to other people, but it shall break in pieces and consume all these kingdoms, and it shall stand for ever.

—Daniel 2:31–44

The chronological and historical fulfillment of the king's dream as explained by Daniel is as follows:

In 538 B.C., after Nebuchadnezzar, king of Babylon, had died and passed from the scene, Belshazzar, a descendant, sat on the throne. As Belshazzar sat at a royal celebration drinking from the vessels that had been taken from the temple, a hand appeared on the wall and wrote, "You are weighed in the balances [scales] and found wanting." That same night a combined army from Media and Persia (present–day Afghanistan and Iran) diverted the Euphrates River, marched under the gates of the city walls, and Babylon (represented by the head of gold on the image) fell to Medo–Persia (represented by the arms and breast of silver on the image).

In 333 B.C., a well–trained Grecian army under the command of a brilliant young general, Alexander, invaded Persia, practically liquidating a million–man Persian army. Persia fell to the Grecian Empire (represented as prophesied by Daniel as the thighs and belly of brass on the image).

In 320 B.C., Alexander died and his empire was divided into four parts, which existed as separate nations. Rome was a republican form of empire that had formed in the Italian peninsula from several different tribes that had settled there in about 500 B.C. after a cessation of intense volcanic activity. Rome defeated the army of Carthage under the leadership of Hannibal around 160 B.C. and moved into the Middle East and absorbed the remains of the Grecian Empire. Rome divided into the Catholic division on the west and the Byzantine division on the east. This was the empire represented by the two legs of iron on Daniel's image.

As prophesied by Daniel, the iron empire, Rome, split into chunks in about A.D. 500, e.g., English Empire, French Empire, German Empire, Dutch Empire, Danish Empire, Spanish Empire, etc. According to Daniel 7:12, this iron empire was to tread down the whole earth and then break the earth in pieces. All of these European empires did indeed tread down the whole earth: all of Europe, Africa, North America, South America, Australia, all the islands, and most of Asia. Then these larger pieces were to be broken into smaller pieces, as indicated in the large iron chunks being broken into smaller chunks in the feet of the image, meaning at the very end of the prophecy, or the very last days.

After WWII, President Franklin Roosevelt and Joseph Stalin met with Winston Churchill in Yalta. Churchill was informed that the European (Roman) colonial empires were finished; they had to give up their colonies. Immediately after WWII, nation after nation joined the United Nations, until there are now over two hundred twenty nations in the world, the majority from the breakup of the Roman colonial system after WWII.

According to Daniel's prophecy, all these nations were to join one union and then one man was to become ruler over this new one–world empire ... the Antichrist. It is beyond doubt that the time is near when this is to happen. This is another irrefutable sign that these are the very last days of the last generation before the Lord returns.

Sign Number 4

Earthquakes in Divers Places

Earthquakes are referenced in the Bible as one of the most judgmental nightmares that can be visited upon mankind. Earthquakes are especially referenced for judgments that will be visited upon those who fight against Jerusalem (Isaiah 29:6–7). In December 2003 there was a severe earthquake in Bam, Iran, that killed at least 30,000, after Ahmadinejad threatened to wipe Israel off the map with an atomic bomb.

All nations in the closing weeks of the Great Tribulation will come against Jerusalem, and it appears that this will be when the earthquake that will move mountains and islands will shake the earth (Zechariah 14:2).

The exponential increase in the number and intensity of earthquakes began once the United Nations (and the Muslim nations involved) began to make the division of Jerusalem a part of a general peace plan for the Middle East.

Without credible controversy, the increase in the number of earthquakes in the past three decades is a dramatic sign that this is indeed the last generation

of the Church Age.

Jesus advised those living in the last days, or the last days of the last days, to be ready for troublesome and dangerous times. He advised us that if the Great Tribulation was to last longer than seven years, no one on earth would be left alive (Matthew 24:22). But even in the generation preceding the Great Tribulation, the years in which you and I live, there would be increasing times of danger, sorrow, and troubles: "And ye shall hear of wars and rumours of wars: . . . For nation shall rise against nation, . . . and there shall be famines, and pestilences, and earthquakes, in divers places. All these are the beginning of sorrows" (Matthew 24:6–8).

Some of the larger earthquakes of history were: A.D. 526, Antioch, Syria, 250,000 deaths; A.D. 1556, Shaanxi, China, 830,000 deaths; A.D. 1737, Calcutta, India, 300,000 deaths. Other earthquakes since A.D. 500 that have claimed as many as 100,000 lives are too numerous to mention. I counted approximately 100 earthquakes in the last century that resulted in the deaths of 1,000 to 100,000. I was at Tang Shan, China, about 70 miles east of Beijing, soon after the earthquake on July 27, 1976, that resulted in the death of 255,000. Deep ditches a mile long were dug and the dead dumped into them without ceremony or notification of relatives. This was to save the lives of survivors from a resulting plague.

The January 2010 earthquake in Haiti was much smaller than the 9.1 in 2004 that actually moved Sumatra out of its geological location. However, the Haiti earthquake demonstrates the catastrophic results that can follow in the wake of even an average 7.0 tremor. A recent news release from Fox indicated that the earth is in an increasing seismic activity period (based on geological evidence). Even in Oklahoma City there has been in 2010 a series of smaller 3.0 to 4.0 earthquakes that have damaged homes.

Are Earthquakes Really Increasing?

Hank Hanegraaff, on his program and in his publication, *Christian Research Journal,* has desperately tried to prove that earthquakes are not increasing to undergird his preterist views. Hank also indicated that those who claim earthquakes are increasing are false prophets. Note the earthquake report by the U.S. Earthquake Information Center from 1987 to 2010, and decide for yourself who is the false prophet. We read in Luke 21:11 that there would not only be an increase in the number of earthquakes, but also an increase in the number of "great earthquakes." This also is certainly true in the last two or three decades.

According to the Bible, earthquakes will continue to increase, both in number and intensity, even moving more islands out of their places: "... and there was a great earthquake, such as was not since men were upon the earth, so mighty an earthquake, and so great.... The cities of the nations fell: ... And every island fled away, and the mountains were not found" (Revelation 16:18–20).

U.S. Geological Survey website, January 15, 2010

Magnitude	1987	1988	1989	1990	1991	1992	1993	1994	1995	1996
8.0–9.9	0	0	1	0	0	0	1	2	3	1
7.0–7.9	11	8	6	12	11	23	15	13	22	21
6.0–6.9	112	93	79	115	105	104	141	161	185	160
5.0–5.9	1,437	1,485	1,444	1,635	1,4;69	1,541	1,449	1,542	1,327	1,223
4.0–4.9	4,146	4,018	4,090	4,493	4,372	5,196	5,034	4,544	8,140	8,794
3.0–3.9	1,806	1,932	2,452	2,457	2,952	4,643	4,263	5,000	5,002	4,869
2.0–2.9	1,037	1,479	1,906	2,364	2,927	3,068	5,390	5,369	3,838	2,388
1.0–1.9	102	118	418	474	801	887	1,177	779	645	295
0.1–0.9	0	3	0	0	1	2	9	17	19	1
No mag.	2,639	3,575	4,189	5,062	3,878	4,084	3,997	1,944	1,826	2,186
Total	11,290	12,711	14,585	16,612	16,516	19,548	21,476	19,371	21,007	19,938
Deaths	1,080	26,552	617	51,916	2,326	3,814	10,036	1,038	7,949	419

Magnitude	1997	1998	1999	2000	2001	2002	2003	2004	2005	2006
8.0–9.9	0	1	0	1	1	0	1	2	1	2
7.0–7.9	20	11	18	14	15	13	14	14	10	9
6.0–6.9	125	117	128	146	121	127	140	141	140	142
5.0–5.9	1,118	979	1,106	1,344	1,224	1,201	1,203	1,515	1,693	1,712
4.0–4.9	7,938	7,303	7,042	8,008	7,991	8,541	8,462	10,888	13,917	12,838
3.0–3.9	4,467	5,945	5,521	4,827	6,266	7,068	7,624	7,932	9,191	9,990
2.0–2.9	2,397	4,091	4,201	3,765	4,164	6,418	7,727	6,316	4,636	4,027
1.0–1.9	388	805	715	1,026	944	1,137	2,506	1,344	26	18
0.1–0.9	4	10	5	5	1	10	134	103	0	2
No mag.	3,415	2,426	2,096	3,120	2,807	2,938	3,608	2,939	864	828
Total	19,872	21,688	20,832	22,256	23,534	27,454	31,419	31,194	30,478	29,568
Deaths	2,907	9,430	22,662	231	21,357	1,685	33,819	228,802	82,364	6,605

* The cited figures were reported January 15, 2010. However, the 2009 and 2010 numbers are as yet incomplete. Deaths from the Haiti earthquake are expected to exceed 200,000.

Magnitude	2007	2008	2009	2010
8.0–9.9	4	0	1	0
7.0–7.9	14	12	16	2
6.0–6.9	178	168	141	7
5.0–5.9	2074	1768	1655	66
4.0–4.9	12078	12291	6877	106
3.0–3.9	9889	11735	2823	17
2.0–2.9	3597	3860	2942	16
1.0–1.9	42	21	26	1
0.1–0.9	2	0	1	0
No mag.	1807	1922	25	1
Total	29685	31777	14507	213
Deaths	712	88011	*1787	*0

SIGN NUMBER 5

EPIDEMIC DISEASES

In the list of last-generation signs that Jesus gave that no one could credibly dispute is the increase of "pestilences." The time frame in which "pestilences" would present a worldwide exponential increase would be just before Christ's return and "the end of the world" (Matthew 24:3). Jesus said of the signs of His coming, **". . . there shall be famines, and pestilences, and earthquakes, in divers places"** (Matthew 24:7). He did not say "maybe" or "perhaps." He said, "there SHALL BE." He didn't say "just in Israel." He said "divers," meaning "many," "countless," "worldwide."

The word "pestilence" is found forty-six times in the Old Testament and two times in the New Testament. The Hebrew *deber* and the Greek *loimos* both mean "plague," or a communicable disease caused by germs infecting entire areas or nations. Pestilences were sent upon all the people living in the land or in the nation. Some pestilences were only three-day epidemics, and others were longer. The Israelites understood that leprosy was a communicable disease. Lepers were to stay outside the camp, or if near the camp, downwind.

It may be argued that cancer, heart disease, and strokes are the main killers of mankind today, but these do not fall into the category of pestilences. You do not catch a heart attack, cancer, or a stroke from another person. At times, God would send a pestilence or a plague upon the fields as a judgment, but these too were caused by microbes. Until about two hundred years ago, until the invention of the microscope, no one knew there were germs or viruses. Nevertheless, it was evident that if sick people with certain types of illnesses were not separated, everyone in the family or community got sick with the same type of illness. In the Book of Leviticus there are fifty-two references to the plague of leprosy and what should be done to prevent the spread of this plague. We read in Numbers 16:49 of 14,700 Israelites who died of a pestilence or plague.

In Bible times, pestilences and plagues were somewhat limited in scope because of limited travel and the distances between populated areas. In the mid–fourteenth century, the silk and spice trade from the Orient brought with it the bubonic or black plague, killing half of the population of Europe. The black plague continued in different places in the world until the beginning of the nineteenth century. It has been estimated that between 20 and 30 million people died of this disease.

Another pestilence was smallpox, which again killed millions in Europe. It was noticed that milkmaids never contracted smallpox. The reason was that those who milk cows contract what is called "cow pox," a mild form of smallpox, and this immunized them against catching the more deadly smallpox. I grew up on a farm and had to milk cows. Later, after I joined the Army, when I was inoculated against smallpox nothing happened. Every move I made to another camp or Army location, I was vaccinated for smallpox again and again, in spite of my protests that I was immune. I must have been vaccinated for smallpox fifteen or more times.

One of the most deadly and far–reaching pandemic diseases (pestilences), one that even claimed more in death than the black plague, was the flu epidemic of 1918. According to the *2009 World Almanac,* the Spanish flu epidemic of 1918 claimed between 50 and 100 million victims. Usually death by influenza is between 8,000 and 30,000 a year. In 2009, in spite of the urgent concerns at the outbreak of the H1N1 (swine) flu, only about 12,000 died as the result of all forms of flu. Influenza, however, remains a serious pandemic disease.

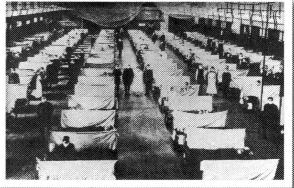

The biblical disease of leprosy also remains defiant to modern medical treatment, although it can be treated with MDT. Leprosy patients worldwide could number as many as 2 million or more. Brazil probably has the highest number—between 50,000 and 100,000.

Malaria is one of the most deadly of the world's pandemic diseases, according to the World Health Organization, infecting as many as 250 million a year, resulting in a million deaths a year. The parasitic disease, which is transmitted by mosquitoes, has developed an increasing immunity to modern medicines. When I lived on the farm, at the age of eight or nine, I suffered from malaria. After a year with quinine, it never returned. However, while serving in the South Pacific,

I always took my Atabrine tablets, even though they turned my fingernails, teeth, and eyes yellow.

According to published statistics, AIDS (originally GRID—Gay Related Immune Deficiency) is one of the worst, if not *the* worst, pandemic and deadly disease of all time. An AIDS victim may spend more than $350,000 in treatment to extend his life by five years. According to the *2009 World Almanac,* as well as numerous other reliable sources, in 2006 there were 34 million known cases of AIDS. There are no current figures as to how many in 2010 would have AIDS, because it is now a politically–protected disease. You can find out how many have died of any disease or accident, but the worldwide homosexual agenda prevents by blackmail or worldview perversion how many have actually died of this loathsome disease, or just how many have it now worldwide. In the United States, the number of known cases ranges from 204 in Wyoming to 88,000 in Florida, and 122,000 in New York. According to Newt Gingrich in his book *Real Change,* AIDS victims from just three counties in Florida in a six–month period hit Medicaid for $487 million. While certain medicines can extend an AIDS victim's life for several years, there is no known cure at this time.

God, in the Bible, explains why this deadly disease threatens entire humanity, and why He had to destroy Sodom and Gomorrah. There is reason to believe that the populations of Sodom and Gomorrah were infected with AIDS.

Jesus Christ warned that pandemic diseases would increase in the last days, and in spite of the advancement in medical science and medical professional services, they continue to increase to worldwide epidemic proportions today. This is an irrefutable sign that these times in which this generation lives are the last days, the last few years preceding the Tribulation period and the Lord's return.

Sign Number 6

Famines

The fact that the word "famine" is found ninety-two times in the Old Testament and seven times in the New Testament would indicate it to be one of the most fearful judgments or catastrophes that could happen to any nation. The fact also that it is mentioned five times more than earthquakes are mentioned would indicate that famines cause more deaths and greater suffering than earthquakes or pandemic diseases. Famines are referenced throughout the Old Testament as occurring in many nations caused by droughts, wars, or insects. Famines are usually mentioned in connection with judgments against nations for sin and revolting against the will of the Lord. We read that in the days of wicked King Ahab of Israel, "... the LORD ... called for a famine ... upon the land seven years" (2 Kings 8:1). Also, we read in Jeremiah 44:13, "... I have punished Jerusalem ... by the famine...." During the Roman siege of Jerusalem in A.D. 70, Josephus reported that the famine was so severe that parents even ate their own children.

During the twentieth century, an estimated 70 million people died from famines across the world, of which an estimated 30 million died during the famine of 1958–61 in China. The other most notable famines of the century included the 1943–45 disaster in Bengal, famines in China in 1928 and 1942, and a sequence of famines in the Soviet Union, including the Holodomor, Stalin's famine, inflicted on Ukraine in 1932–33.

A few of the great famines of the late twentieth century were: the Biafran famine in the 1960s, the disaster in Cambodia in the 1970s, the Ethiopian famine of

1983–85, and the North Korean famine of the 1990s.

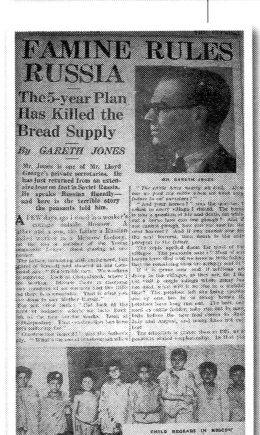

The largest famine of the twentieth century, and almost certainly of all time, was the 1958–61 Great Leap Forward famine of China. The immediate cause of this famine lay in Chairman Mao Tse-tung's ill-fated attempt to transform China from an agricultural nation. Communist Party cadres across China insisted that peasants abandon their farms for collective farms and begin to produce steel in small foundries, often melting down their farm instruments in the process.

The Manmade Famine of 1932–33, artificially organized by Stalin's regime, was one of the most tragic pages in the history of the Ukrainian nation. According to various sources, from 7 to 10 million people died of starvation. Every Ukrainian family suffered from that famine.

In 1984 a famine ravaged Ethiopia, killing over one million. The prime minister of Ethiopia, Meles Zenawi, said it was a nightmare too horrible to even describe. In the fall of 2002 another famine hit Ethiopia that was even more devastating than the first.

During a six-year drought in Kenya that lasted from 2000 to 2006, so many died that no count was possible. According to the May 20, 2006, edition of *The Independent,* trees in many areas were garnished with hanging bodies. Men who could not stand to see their livestock, wives, and children dying of hunger hanged themselves. According to the November 22, 2002, edition of the *Nepali Times,* over 800,000 citizens of Nepal had left their homes searching for food. One witness said, "We are all going to starve to death this year, that's for sure."

Having been to China many times, I have heard many disturbing stories about how cities were emptied and even college students were taken from homes and trucked to Inner Mongolia to take care of their own needs in the fierce winters, without adequate housing. Most died of hunger or froze to death. After 1917, the same tragedy occurred in the communization of Ukraine where from 10 to 20 million died from hunger. In Cambodia, the Marxist Pol Pot emptied the cities and one-half the population was executed or died from hunger. My wife Kim's parents died from hunger in Phnom Phen, and seven of her brothers and sisters died in the Killing Fields. One sister's family was buried alive.

Here in the United States the threat of famine seems to be something that occurred in Bible times or in storybooks that have long gone out of print. The reason is that Americans have never really had to be concerned with famines. God has indeed blessed this nation "from sea to shining sea" because we honored Him in our homes, schools, and churches. But our nation today is being ruled by men and women who know not God. They have legislated God out of our schools. Our homes, if they can be called homes, are mostly broken, with only one parent and no Bible, devotion, or prayer. Our churches are now pastored by men who are more concerned with music and numbers than they are with "thus saith the Lord." Without government and political figures politicizing God's creation with lies and financial schemes, how long will the Creator remain silent?

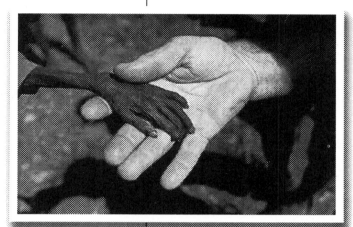

Jesus gave this generation a sign: "And great earthquakes shall be in divers places, and *famines*, and pestilences . . ." (Luke 21:11).

The rider of the black horse of Revelation 6:5–6 is ready to ride across America: "And when he had opened the third seal, I heard the third beast say, Come and see. And I beheld, and lo a black horse; and he that sat on him had a pair of balances in his hand. And I heard a voice in the midst of the four beasts say, A measure of wheat for a penny, and three measures of barley for a penny; and see thou hurt not the oil and the wine."

Some believe that the United States is referenced in Revelation 18:8 after the church is gone: "Therefore shall her plagues come in one day, death, and mourning, and famine; and she shall be utterly burned with fire: for strong is the Lord God who judgeth her."

This is just one more reason why Christians today need to pray for our nation according to 2 Chronicles 7:14: "If my people, which are called by my name, shall humble themselves, and pray, and seek my face, and turn from their wicked ways; then will I hear from heaven, and will forgive their sin, and will heal their land."

Sign Number 7

Wars and

Rumors of Wars

Included in the signs that God would give the last generation before the Tribulation affecting the physical status of mankind was the increase of war and rumors of war.

> And ye shall hear of wars and rumours of wars: see that ye be not troubled: for all these things must come to pass, but the end is not yet. For nation shall rise against nation, and kingdom against kingdom: and there shall be famines, and pestilences, and earthquakes, in divers places.
>
> —Matthew 24:6–7

Of the four major judgments of the human race (earthquakes, famine, pestilences, wars), war is the most persistent and disastrous. War is referenced in the Bible more than two hundred times. War is not a judgment of nature, but man bringing judgment upon himself. "From whence come wars and fightings among you? come they not hence, even of your lusts that war in your members?" (James 4:1).

Man's savagery and inhumanity toward or against each other far exceeds that of the beast kingdom. It is unimaginable how mankind could exalt its own estate if only wars could have been abolished. If this majority of man's effort wasted in the manufacturing of war machines, the maintaining of armies, and the development of defenses could have been directed to more constructive social and economic projects, we can only think what this world would be like today. Behind all this hatred and fighting of man against man has been Satan in his vain jealousy to exalt his own kingdom above the Kingdom of God. Jesus warned that just before He returned that wars would increase, because as we read in Revelation 12:12, "... Woe to the inhabiters of the earth and of the sea! for the devil is come down unto you, having great wrath, because he knoweth that he hath but a short time."

Forty years after Jesus foretold what would come to pass before He returned to put down all the wars of mankind, Jerusalem was destroyed and the Jews left alive were scattered into all nations. The wars of Rome in maintaining the outreach of their vast empire in Europe and Asia continued. These were followed by the Islamic wars against the Byzantine Empire, then the Mongol invasion of Genghis Khan from the East, then the colonial empire wars of Africa, North America, South America, and the Far East. Continuing at the same time were the wars between England, France, and Germany, interspersed with the American Revolution, the French Revolution, and the American Civil War, with other regional wars too numerous to mention. But Jesus said that as the time of His coming again drew near, there would be world wars of nation against nation and kingdom against kingdom.

In 1914 Germany invaded France, and armies from nations on every continent became involved in a conflict that lasted until 1918. After World War One, the League of Nations was founded to prevent war between nations and another world war, but the United States voted not to be involved and its influence in negotiations of international differences between nations was minimal and ineffective.

In September of 1939 Germany invaded Poland. France and England declared a state of war with Germany, and when Japan attacked the United States in December 1941, the war had spread to all six continents once more. As Jesus prophesied, kingdom was again at war with kingdom.

World War Two ended in Europe in the summer of 1945

with the final defeat of Germany by the Allied forces of England and the United States and the army of Russia advancing from the east. The Pacific arena of World War Two ended in August 1945 with the dropping of two atomic bombs on Japan.

In 1945 the United Nations was formed to prevent future conflict, as President Franklin Roosevelt said, the end to all wars. Yet as Jesus indicated, wars have continued to this present time.

No period has witnessed the escalation of wars as has the twentieth century. The Red Cross has estimated that over 100 million people have been killed in wars since the twentieth century began. Up until 1914, war had never been universal, but in both World Wars One and Two, total war was waged.

Since World War Two, the war that was supposed to make the world safe for democracy, there have been numerous major wars and hundreds of rebellions and revolutions. The death toll in conflicts since the end of World War Two has now topped 23 million.

Korean War (1950–1953). To placate Russia, Korea was divided into two nations in the peace treaty following World War Two. North Korea attacked South Korea with the United States Army supporting the army of South Korea.

Vietnam War (1959–1975). As with the division of Vietnam into two political entities, war between the two entities resulted in the communist North trying to conquer the free southern entity. This emerged into the longest war the U.S. had ever fought to that time.

Persian Gulf War (1991–Present). The involvement of United States forces first in Iraq and later in Afghanistan has been a deadly and costly sideshow to the continuing goals of Islam to make all the world submit to subjection under the Islamic religion.

The United Nations defines "major wars" as military conflicts inflicting one thousand battlefield deaths per year. In 1965, there were ten major wars under way. Wars and the ravages of civil distress are affecting millions worldwide. There were thirty–five ongoing conflicts at the end of 2003. The millennium ended with much of the world consumed in armed conflict or cultivating an uncertain peace.

Since the end of the Cold War more conflicts have ended in negotiated settlements than in victory. Conflicts that end in negotiated settlements are far more likely to restart than those that end in victory.

In 2010 the threat of Iran to destroy Israel with nuclear weapons that are in the development stage poses a real threat to world peace and threatens another war in which Russia and China may be involved. There are daily rumors about developments that relate to the war between Gog and Magog of Ezekiel 38–39.

Surely the continuing wars with kingdom against kingdom will not end until Jesus Christ returns at the Battle of Armageddon, which may be sooner than the sleeping church members today think.

Major A.D. Wars

Lowest Estimate	Event	Location	From	To
3,000,000–7,000,000	Yellow Turban Rebellion	China	184	205
33,000,000–36,000,000	An Shi Rebellion	China	756	763
30,000,000–40,000,000	Mongol Conquests	Asia, Central and Eastern Europe, Middle East	1207	1472
15,000,000–20,000,000	Conquests of Timur	Middle East, India, Central Asia, Russia	1369	1405
2,000,000–4,000,000	French Wars of Religion	France	1562	1598
25,000,000	Qing dynasty conquest of the Ming dynasty	China	1616	1662
3,000,000–11,500,000	Thirty Years' War	Holy Roman Empire	1618	1648
3,500,000–6,500,000	Napoleonic Wars	Europe, Atlantic, Pacific, and Indian Oceans	1804	1815
2,000,000	Shaka's conquests	Africa	1816	1828
20,000,000–30,000,000	Taiping Rebellion	China	1851	1864
8,000,000–12,000,000	Muslim Rebellion	China	1862	1877
15,000,000–65,000,000 (includes Spanish flu deaths)	World War I	Worldwide	1914	1919
5,000,000–9,000,000	Russian Civil War	Russia	1917	1921
40,000,000–72,000,000	World War II	Worldwide	1939	1945
2,500,000–3,500,000	Korean War	Korean Peninsula	1950	1953
2,495,000–5,020,000	Vietnam War	Southeast Asia	1959	1975
1,500,000–2,000,000	Afghan Civil War	Afghanistan	1979	Present
400,000–2,000,000	Iran–Iraq War	Iran, Iraq	1980	1988
3,800,000–5,400,000	Second Congo War	Democratic Republic of the Congo	1998	2003

Sign Number 8

Signs in Calendar Mathematics

The mathematical patterns and compositions of chromosomes in DNA was first established in God's creation in every form of life.

A new human being is determined by twenty–three chromosomes from the father and twenty–three chromosomes from the mother. Just one chromosome determines whether the new human being will be male or female. Some plants have hundreds of chromosomes, yet if even one chromosome is out of order, that plant will not reproduce.

The Scriptures say that even the days are numbered.

» God told Moses Israel could not enter the Promised Land on the 9th of Av.
» The first temple was destroyed by the Babylonians on the 9th of Av, 586 B.C.
» The second temple was destroyed by the Romans on the 9th of Av, A.D. 70.
» The decree to expel the Jews from England was on the 9th of Av, 1290.
» The Spanish Inquisition order for Jews was on the 9th of Av, 1492.
» World War One began on the 9th of Av, 1914.
» Hitler's order to kill all the Jews in Warsaw was issued on the 9th of Av, 1942.
» Jewish settlers were expelled from Gaza on the 9th of Av, 2006.

In Scripture, forty is the number of probationary judgment:

» Nineveh—forty days to repent
» Israel—in Egypt four hundred years
» Israel—in the wilderness forty years
» The flood—rained for forty days
» From Adam to Jesus—who was judged in man's place, was four thousand years

On pages 139–141 of my book *God the Master Mathematician,* I quote Edward Gibbons from the second volume of *The Decline and Fall of the Roman Empire,* written in 1776, where Irenæus, Justin Martyr, and others actually conversed with those who had been taught by the apostles of Jesus that inasmuch as the creation was completed in six days, and one day is with the Lord as a thousand years, this age would end in six thousand years, and then the Tribulation would come. But the Christians alive at that time would escape this time of trouble. The Tribulation would then be followed by a Sabbath of one thousand years.

Gibbons went on to say that this teaching was regretfully changed to an allegorical story by the church, meaning the Catholic Church.

We are now at the end of six thousand years.

Six days shall work be done: but the seventh day is the sabbath of rest, an holy convocation; ye shall do no work therein: it is the sabbath of the LORD in all your dwellings.

Leviticus 23:3

But, beloved, be not ignorant of this one thing, that one day is with the Lord as a thousand years, and a thousand years as one day.

—2 Peter 3:8

In Matthew 24:37 we read, "But as the days of Noe were, so shall also the coming of the Son of man be." And in Genesis 6:1 we read, ". . . men began to multiply on the face of the earth. . . ." Lambert Dolphin estimated that there were 9 billion people on earth at the time of the flood. The population today is close to 7 billion.

Man was created on the sixth day of creation; he is appointed six decades to live; he is to be buried in a six-foot grave; and the number of man is 666 (Revelation 13:18). The dispensational course of time is to be seven thousand years, with the Lord's Day being the last one thousand (Revelation 20:3). It appears conclusive that Ussher's chronology indicates man's six days (six thousand years) would have ended at A.D. 2000. However, is God giving this present generation forty probationary years as He did Israel? Or an entire generation of Israel of seventy years after the birth of Jesus Christ? Many today consider A.D. 2012 the end of this age due to the Mayan calendar ending on this year. We know that Ussher's chronology of years was off by four years, and it could have been off possibly even more.

In any event, calendar mathematics indicates that man's day is about up. While we do not set dates for the Lord's return, we are convinced the time is near, very near, for the Lord's return.

Sign Number 9

When Towers Fall

The first city tower constructed, according to the Bible, was the Tower of Babel. The biblical account of the tower and its fall is recorded in Genesis 11:1–9:

> And the whole earth was of one language, and of one speech. And it came to pass, as they journeyed from the east, that they found a plain in the land of Shinar; and they dwelt there. And they said one to another, Go to, let us make brick, and burn them throughly. And they had brick for stone, and slime had they for morter. And they said, Go to, let us build us a city and a tower, whose top may reach unto heaven; and let us make us a name, lest we be scattered abroad upon the face of the whole earth. And the LORD came down to see the city and the tower, which the children of men builded. And the LORD said, Behold, the people is one, and they have all one language; and this they begin to do: and now nothing will be restrained from them, which they have imagined to do. Go to, let us go down, and there confound their language, that they may not understand one another's speech. So the LORD scattered them abroad from thence upon the face of all the earth: and they left off to build the city. Therefore is the name of it called Babel; because the LORD did there confound the language of all the earth: and from thence did the LORD scatter them abroad upon the face of all the earth.

This was not a tower erected to the glory of God, but rather to the glory of man. The people themselves decided, "Let us build us a city"; "Let us make us a name." The tower has also been called the tower of Nimrod, because Nimrod was evidently the king or leader of the people at that time.

Other than just a matter of pride, it could be suggested that fear was also a motivating factor. The tower was evidently built in the days of Peleg. God willed that the descendants of the flood survivors spread out and take dominion of the earth, but this did not seem to be the plan of Nimrod. Therefore, we read in Genesis 10:25 that the EARTH was divided. The Hebrew word for earth here, and some seven hundred times in the Old Testament, is *erets*, and it always means ground, dirt, landmass. As a consequence of evidently breaking the landmass of the planet into continents and islands, we read in Genesis 10:32, "... were the nations divided in the earth after the flood."

We are not told how high the Tower of Babel got before God confounded the language of the builders. But we can, however, understand their motivation. If the landmass was breaking up and separating, they might have concluded that building a skyscraper to the heavens was their only way of saving the human race. If this were happening today, the nations would probably try to launch space ships to save the human remnant.

In anticipation of building a very high tower, we read that they "burned the bricks throughly." Babylon was a continuance of Babel, and when I was in Babylon in 1978 I took note that the bricks of the old city were still extremely hard, solid, and appeared as if they had just come out of the kiln, even though they were forty-three hundred years old, or older. In fact, some may actually have been used in the original Tower of Babel.

The construction and end of the Babel project is noted in the following traditional and historical sources:

Destruction
The account in Genesis makes no mention of any destruction of the tower. The people whose languages are confounded simply stop building their city, and are scattered from there over the face of the earth. However, in other sources such as the Book of Jubilees (10:18–27), Cornelius Alexander (frag. 10), Abydenus (frags. 5 and 6), Josephus (Antiquities 1.4.3), and the Sibylline Oracles (iii. 117–129), God overturns the tower with a great wind. In the Midrash, it said that the top of the tower was burnt, the bottom was swallowed, and the middle was left standing to erode over time. . . .

Book of Jubilees
The Book of Jubilees contains one of the most detailed accounts found anywhere of the Tower.

"And they began to build, and in the fourth week they made brick with fire, and the bricks served them for stone, and the clay with which they cemented them together was asphalt which comes out of the sea, and out of the fountains of water in the land of Shinar. And they built it: forty and three years were they building it; its breadth was 203 bricks, and the height [of a brick] was the third of one; its height amounted to 5433 cubits and 2 palms, and [the extent of one wall was] thirteen stades [and of the other thirty stades]" (Jubilees 10:20–21, Charles' 1913 translation)

The Book of Jubilees recounts Genesis and the first twelve chapters of Exodus, elaborating on the text (similar to a Midrash). It is often categorized as one of the Pseudepigrapha and dated to the late 2nd century B.C., but it is still in the canon of the Ethiopian Orthodox Tewahedo Church.

Josephus' Antiquities of the Jews

The Jewish historian and Roman citizen Flavius Josephus, in his *Antiquities of the Jews* (c. A.D. 94), recounted history as found in the Hebrew Bible and mentioned the Tower of Babel. He wrote that it was Nimrod who had the tower built and that Nimrod was a tyrant who tried to turn the people away from God. In this account, God confused the people rather than destroying them because destroying people with a flood hadn't taught them to be godly. . . .

Midrash

Rabbinic literature offers many different accounts of other causes for building the Tower of Babel, and of the intentions of its builders. The Mishnah (the first written record of the Jewish oral law, c. A.D. 200) describes the Tower as a rebellion against God. Some later Midrash record that the builders of the Tower, called "the generation of secession" in the Jewish sources, said: "God has no right to choose the upper world for Himself, and to leave the lower world to us; therefore we will build us a tower, with an idol on the top holding a sword, so that it may appear as if it intended to war with God" (Gen. R. xxxviii. 7; Tan., ed. Buber, Noah, xxvii. et seq.).

The building of the Tower was meant to bid defiance not only to God, but also to Abraham, who exhorted the builders to reverence. The passage mentions that the builders spoke sharp words against God, not cited in the Bible, saying that once every 1,656 years, heaven tottered so that the water poured down upon the earth, therefore they would support it by columns that there might not be another deluge (Gen. R. l.c.; Tan. l.c.; similarly Josephus, "Ant." i. 4, § 2).

Some among that sinful generation even wanted to war against

God in heaven (Talmud Sanhedrin 109a.) They were encouraged in this wild undertaking by the notion that arrows which they shot into the sky fell back dripping with blood, so that the people really believed that they could wage war against the inhabitants of the heavens (Sefer ha-Yashar, Noah, ed. Leghorn, 12b). According to Josephus and Midrash Pirke R. El. xxiv., it was mainly Nimrod who persuaded his contemporaries to build the Tower, while other rabbinical sources assert, on the contrary, that Nimrod separated from the builders. . . .

Qur'an and Islamic traditions

Though not mentioned by name, the Qur'an has a story with similarities to the biblical story of the Tower of Babel, though set in the Egypt of Moses. In Suras 28:38 and 40:36–37, Pharaoh asks Haman to build him a stone, or clay tower so that he can mount up to heaven and confront the God of Moses.

Another story in Sura 2:102 mentions the name of Babil, but tells of when Jin taught the people of Babylon the tricks of magic and warned them that magic is a sin and that their teaching them magic is a test of faith. A tale about Babil appears more fully in the writings of Yaqut (i, 448 f.) and the Lisan el-'Arab (xiii. 72), but without the tower: mankind were swept together by winds into the plain that was afterward called "Babil," where they were assigned their separate languages by Allah, and were then scattered again in the same way.

In *The History of the Prophets and Kings* by the ninth century Muslim historian al-Tabari, a fuller version is given: Nimrod has the tower built in Babil, Allah destroys it, and the language of mankind, formerly Syriac, is then confused into 72 languages. Another Muslim historian of the thirteenth century, Abu al-Fida relates the same story, adding that the patriarch Eber (an ancestor of Abraham) was allowed to keep the original tongue, Hebrew in this case, because he would not partake in the building.

Though variations of the stories similar to the Judeo-Christian narrative of the Tower of Babel exist within Islamic traditions, the central theme of Allah separating humankind on the basis of language is alien to Islam according to author Yahya Emmerick. In Islamic belief Allah created nations to know each other and not to be separated....

In Western culture

Historical linguistics has long wrestled with the idea of a single original language. In the Middle Ages, and down to the seventeenth century, attempts were made to identify a living descendent of the Adamic language, e.g. in the Irish legend of Fenius Farsa.

Pieter Brueghel's influential portrayal is based on the Colosseum in Rome, while later conical depictions of the tower (as depicted in Doré's illustration) resemble much later Muslim towers observed by nineteenth century explorers in the area, notably the Minaret of Samarra. M. C. Escher depicts a more stylized geometrical structure in his woodcut representing the story....

—Wikipedia.org, "Tower of Babel"

In the Old Testament we read that many kings erected their own identifying towers, just as Nimrod built his. However, like Nimrod's tower, these towers were erected for self–glory, and sooner or later all were destroyed except what foundational evidences remain today, and certainly there is no glory in these meager scattered stones.

Tower of London

William the Conqueror built the Tower of London in A.D. 1078. The Tower included a complex of several buildings, probably no more than one hundred feet high. It has been used during the reign of England's kings and queens for many purposes. One of those purposes was a prison for enemies of the crown. Through succeeding centuries, the warning, "Be careful, or you will go to the Tower," filled Englishmen with deadly fear. King Henry VIII used the Tower as a holding place for some of his wives until he could present excuses for having them beheaded in the courtyard.
Parts of the Tower today are used as a museum, which I have visited several times. But the Tower itself presents no citizens a reason for glory due to its association with some of the most horrible crimes in history.

Eiffel Tower

The Eiffel Tower is a nineteenth century iron lattice tower located on the Champ de Mars in Paris that has become both a global icon of France

and one of the most recognizable structures in the world. The Eiffel Tower, which is the tallest building in Paris, is the single most visited paid monument in the world; millions of people ascend it every year. Named after its designer, engineer Gustave Eiffel, the tower was built as the entrance arch for the 1889 World's Fair.

The tower stands at 324 meters (1,063 feet) tall, about the same height as an eighty–one–story building. It was the tallest structure in the world from its completion until 1930, when it was eclipsed by the Chrysler Building in New York City. Not including broadcast antennas, it is the second–tallest structure in France, behind the Millau Viaduct, completed in 2004.

The tower has become the most prominent symbol of both Paris and France, often in the establishing shot of movies set in the city.

Built in the 1800s, the Eiffel Tower was to commemorate the glory of France during the colonial expansion period and the reign of Napoleon. However, France today is just another member of the European Union, unable to retain anything more than an image of its golden years, humbled by World War One and completely embarrassed by its total collapse in only a week to the German army in World War Two. The Eiffel Tower stands as a lonely sentinel and a hollow reminder of the glory that once was.

Empire State Building

The United States entered the tower competition in 1931 with the erection of the Empire State Building. Including its spire, the total height was 1,454 feet. Upon its completion, it was named as one of the Seven Wonders of the World. Its completion, however, came at the height of the Great Depression, and due to high rent problems, it remained practically empty during the Great Depression years. It became known as "the killing tower," as many during the Depression era paid to ride to the 102nd floor, where they promptly took the faster and cheaper way down . . . by jumping to the street below.

The owners did recoup some of their losses by renting it to moviemakers for flicks like *King Kong,* who while clasping the heroine in his monstrous claws, fought off the entire U.S. Army and Air Force.

Willis (Sears) Tower

The Sears Tower, as it was first known, was completed in 1974 and remained the world's tallest building until 1998, standing at a height, including spire, of 1,730 feet (approximately one–third of a mile). At the time, Sears was the largest retailer in the world, with 350,000 employees. It was built for, and used almost entirely by the Sears Corporation (formerly Sears and Roebuck). Sears, a U.S.A.-based manufacturer and retailer, was known as a quality provider for clothing, televisions, radios, farming equipment, appliances, furniture, tools, etc. My wife and I still have a Sears refrigerator in our kitchen. In Oklahoma City, Sears built a huge outlet complex at the corner of 23rd and Pennsylvania in the late 1950s. However, in the early 1990s this huge, beautiful building was torn down.

The program of a global economy and a global government proposed and promoted by the Council on Foreign Relations since its formation in 1918 after the United States rejected any alliance with the League of Nations began to be enacted. Controlling the news media and the political process, David Rockefeller and his three thousand CFR comrades sold U.S. sovereignty and our free enterprise system for nothing more than a seat in a one-world social order where Americans are outvoted two hundred to one by Communists, Buddhists, Hindus, and Muslims.

By removing all trade barriers, import taxes, and embargo restrictions, billions of tons of foreign goods, merchandise, and produce, are either made or grown by 5 billion foreigners, the majority of whom are working for less than a dollar an hour. New retail entities like Wal-Mart, Target, and others began satisfying greedy U.S. buyers with cheaper goodies from all over the world. Traditional U.S. retail corporations like Sears, Montgomery Ward, J. C. Penney, and others, either went bankrupt or had to greatly reduce employees, stores, and outreach. President Bill Clinton did delay the death throes of the U.S. economy by getting legislation passed to use banking funds like savings, 401Ks, stocks, and other mediums of exchange, to build millions of new homes. For several years, the electricians, carpenters, plumbers, and real estate companies were busy, but then someone had to be put into the houses. Most of those who got the houses that Bill built were those who could not pay for them, including 5 million illegal immigrants. As Bill was warned, in 2008 the banks had no money. The economy froze. In the wings waiting to take over was a neo-Marxist by the name of Barack Obama.

Today, the Sears Tower in Chicago, the tallest building in the world until 1998, serves as a tombstone for the graveyard of the American free enterprise system.

THE WORLD TRADE TOWERS

The World Trade Towers in Lower Manhattan, New York City, were completed in 1971. The Sears Tower was actually three feet higher (with spire), yet the Twin Towers were the best-known and most publicized buildings in the world, reaching a height of 1,727 feet, including spire. I was privileged to enjoy dinner in the North Tower, top floor restau-

rant, on two occasions. The view at night of the entire New York City complex, and looking east over Long Island, was unbelievable.

Most of us can remember where we were and what we were doing when memorable events occur. I can remember exactly where I was and what I was doing when the Japanese bombed Pearl Harbor. On the morning of September 11, 2001, I had decided to take a day off at the ministry and go fishing with an old buddy, Daryl Robison, at Texoma Lake, about one hundred twenty miles south of Oklahoma City. Just before we arrived at our favorite fishing spot, my office called to inform me that something terrible had happened in New York City. We were being attacked and already two airliners had plunged into the Twin Towers. Later we were informed another plane had hit the Pentagon in Washington, D.C. Realizing that even if this was the start of another world war, or even the end of the world, there was nothing we could do about it, we continued to the lake and fished until noon. The fish were not biting anyway, so we pulled up our lines and headed back. On the way back, lines of cars were backed up at the service stations, evidently fearing what had happened might shut off foreign gasoline supplies. Later that night after we

had returned home, the television showed crowds in Muslim capitols around the world celebrating the destruction of the Twin Towers and the deaths of almost three thousand people, which included employees, policemen, and firefighters. To most of the Muslim world this was not just the destruction of several buildings in New York City; it was the triumph of Islam over so-called Christian America.

The 767s that were flown into the buildings had just been filled with fuel, and the films of the catastrophe shown later showed helpless victims plunging to their deaths to escape the terrible heat. This was a reminder that Hell would doubtless be a thousand times hotter, yet so few think about spending eternity there. Also in seeing the entire scenario of the planes hitting the buildings, the resulting fires, and then the mysterious collapse of the buildings destroying the entire seven-building complex, to me at least was beyond understanding. Many have theorized or tried to explain that this seemingly mysterious aftermath was caused by an extended internal or external conspiracy. Regardless, whatever occurred in the catastrophic events that followed the planes hitting the building, we must leave to the providence of God.

The strange desire for men to build towers reaching into the heavens, beginning at Babel, is inspired by the god of this world who said, ". . . I will exalt my throne above the stars of God . . ." (Isaiah 14:13).

Tower of Dubai

The latest and highest tower to exalt man's kingdom above the stars of God is the Burj Khalifa, also called the Tower of Dubai, on the Persian Gulf, the pride of the Islamic world. The Muslim world is now claiming that this tower proves that their god is greater than the God of Christians. However, according to God's Word, there will be earthquakes so great in the coming Tribulation that mountains will be leveled, islands moved out of their places, and even every wall built by man will fall (Ezekiel 38:20; Revelation 16:18).

The Dubai Tower was finished on January 4, 2010, reaching a height of 2,717 feet, over one–half mile, with elevators that travel forty miles an hour. But God says that like the Tower of Babel, and the World Trade Center, this tower also will fall:

> And there shall be upon every high mountain, and upon every high hill, rivers and streams of waters in the day of the great slaughter, **when the towers fall.** Moreover the light of the moon shall be as the light of the sun, and the light of the sun shall be sevenfold, as the light of seven days, in the day that the LORD bindeth up the breach of his people, and healeth the stroke of their wound. Behold, the name of the LORD cometh from far, burning with his anger, and the burden thereof is heavy: his lips are full of indignation, and his tongue as a devouring fire.
>
> —Isaiah 30:25–27

The erection of towers today and their resulting fate is another sign that these are indeed the last days of the last days.

Sign Number 10

As It Was In the Days of Noah

In Luke 17:20 we read that Jesus was confronted with the question of "when the kingdom of God should come." Jesus avoided the question directly by responding to His disciples in Luke 17:22–27:

And he said unto the disciples, The days will come, when ye shall desire to see one of the days of the Son of man, and ye shall not see it. And they shall say to you, See here; or, See there: go not after them, nor follow them. For as the lightning, that lighteneth out of the one part under heaven, shineth unto the other part under heaven; so shall also the Son of man be in his day. But first must he suffer many things, and be rejected of this generation. And as it was in the days of Noe, so shall it be also in the days of the Son of man. They did eat, they drank, they married wives, they were given in marriage, until the day that Noe entered into the ark, and the flood came, and destroyed them all.

The condition of mankind in the world before the flood:

1. The human race had multiplied over the face of the earth from 4004

B.C. to 2349 B.C., from the first man (Adam) and the first woman (Eve), to a population estimated somewhere between 6 billion and 12 billion. This exponential increase over sixteen hundred years was due to men and women living hundreds of years. Methusaleh lived to the age of nine hundred sixty–nine years.

2. Violence filled the earth, because there was no governmental authority, and every man did what he thought was right in his own eyes. There was no penalty for theft, sexual crimes, assault, or murder.

3. According to Genesis 6, there was a spiritual invasion of the "sons of God," whom most traditional Bible scholars have understood to be angels who married women.

4. Men and women were not interested in God's will for their lives or His Word, as Noah preached for one hundred twenty years and evidently did not win one soul to the Lord outside his immediate family.

5. Every man and woman alive at that time, other than the eight members of Noah's family, were drowned in a worldwide flood.

Of course, we understand there could be many parallels or differences in the environment, but Jesus did not indicate these conditions would be the same when He came again. He references only the people, their social order, and their way of life.

As It Is in the Days of Noah Hutchings

1. The human race has multiplied again over the face of the earth, in spite of wars, natural disasters, pandemic diseases, and famines. The current population of the earth is approaching 7 billion, comparable to what it was before the flood.

2. According to the U.S. Census Bureau (June 25, 2010), the population of the United States is 309,563,823. The arrests for crimes committed for 2008, the latest year statistics were available, was 10,662,208. Of these arrests, over 536,000 were arrests for violent crimes, including murder, yet there were only thirty–six executions. In many states now, laws have been passed to forbid executions even for mass murder. There are no available statistics for world crime, yet the death penalty is now forbidden in most countries. Turkey applied for membership in the

European Union, but was turned down because that nation still has the death penalty for murder. As it was before the flood, people do what is right for themselves. If it makes them feel good, they do it with less penalty for their crimes.

3. Paul wrote in his first letter to Timothy, chapter 4, verse 1, "Now the Spirit speaketh expressly, that in the latter times some shall depart from the faith, giving heed to seducing spirits. . . ." Whether a continuing report from around the world of UFO sightings is a fulfillment of Paul's writing is a matter of opinion, but it is evident that many of our churches are departing from the faith once delivered to the saints and being seduced by all kinds of false and satanic doctrines.

4. The Bible has been published in every language known to man. The Gospel offering every person on planet earth the opportunity to be saved from sin and receive the gift of eternal life from God through faith in Jesus Christ is broadcast and telecast every minute of the day. In most cities there is a church on almost every corner, yet fewer are coming to the knowledge of the truth and being saved.

5. According to 1 Thessalonians 4:13–18, the church (every person in the world who is a Christian) will be taken out of this world suddenly, and as with those left behind after Noah and his family entered the ark, ". . . sudden destruction cometh upon them, as travail upon a woman with child; and they shall not escape" (1 Thessalonians 5:3).

As Jesus said, the world today in many ways is just like it was before the flood, and in this we know, these are the last days of the last days.

SIGN NUMBER 11

THE WORLDVIEW THEORY OF EVOLUTION

The concept, idea, theory, or the imagination that the millions of forms of conscious life today somehow began with spontaneous chemical actions millions or billions of years ago is the basis for the worldview of evolution that is universally accepted in the twenty–first century. This theory is what man himself imagines concerning how he began when he will not accept the biblical record and the testimony of nature that all living things were brought into being at the same time by a very special Creator. If man accepts that he was created, then he is responsible to that Creator. This moral responsibility to higher authority was rejected by the Antediluvians who then came up with the idea of evolution. In Romans 1, we read:

18: For the wrath of God is revealed from heaven against all ungodliness and unrighteousness of men, who hold the truth in unrighteousness;

19: Because that which may be known of God is manifest in them; for God hath shewed it unto them.

20: For the invisible things of him from the creation of the world are clearly seen, being understood by the things that are made, even his eternal power and Godhead; so that they are without excuse:

21: Because that, when they knew God, they glorified him not as God, neither were thankful; but became vain in their imaginations, and their

foolish heart was darkened.

22: Professing themselves to be wise, they became fools,

23: And changed the glory of the uncorruptible God into an image made like to corruptible man, and to birds, and fourfooted beasts, and creeping things.

24: Wherefore God also gave them up to uncleanness through the lusts of their own hearts, to dishonour their own bodies between themselves:

25: Who changed the truth of God into a lie, and worshipped and served the creature more than the Creator, who is blessed for ever. Amen.

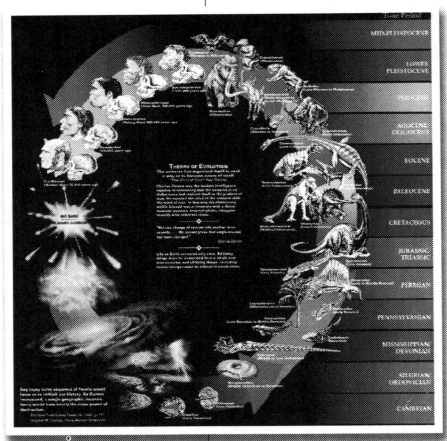

The primary reference in the preceding scripture passage indicates Paul included first the generation of mankind that was lost in the flood. We think of the theory of evolution, also known as the theory of natural selection, as being proposed in Darwin's book, *Origin of Species*, 1889, of being a recent scientific conclusion. But it is neither recent nor scientific. According to the *Internet Encyclopedia of Philosophy*, Aristotle classified the successive order of living beings in his *scala naturae* (Great Chain of Beings). Inasmuch as the Antediluvians refused to believe in a Creator, they worshipped the lower forms of life more than God. Even after the appearance of the Creator upon the earth, the theory of evolution had its disciples even through the Middle Ages like Erigena and Nicholas of Cusa. Darwin simply put a more precise chronology on the so–called different successive spirals of the ideas of evolutionary life forms of his predecessors.

Adolf Hitler was a Darwinian disciple; he simply wanted to help evolution along by eliminating the lower inferior humans. Westcott and Hort, translators of the two Alexandrian texts that are the base texts for most new version Bibles, were Darwinian scholars. Hort said that the black race was just a step up from a Newfoundland dog.

There is an adage that the more a man is educated, the more he knows that he doesn't know. To me, at least, it is beyond imagination how a mindless chemical action could have ever produced me, with such parts like eyes, nose, ears, and a brain with complicated functions so intricate that no one has been able to explain. Yet evolution today is taught in all levels of education universally and only a very few pastors dare to challenge it from the pulpit, even though men like Bill Gates, Dr. Steven Meyer, and others prove that DNA has to be a formatted–creation–produced–design more complicated than the most advanced computer program.

Like the Antediluvians, the generation today in "vain imaginations" deny their responsibility to God their Creator and profess they came from creeping things, to birds, then beasts, and from beasts (apes), to humans. This generation has changed the "truth of God into a lie" rather than to serve their Creator.

Jesus said that as it was in the days of Noah, before the flood, so it would be when He came again. Because our governmental education system, and even the preachers, are either rejecting or ignoring books like *The Cell* and DVDs like *Miracle of Life,* produced in 2009, God will destroy this generation as He did the one before the flood and for the same reason. The world acceptance of evolution as the reason for our being is another important sign that Jesus is coming soon.

Sign Number 12

Exponential Homosexual Relationships and Activity

Man is a *homo* animal. Animal means animated, or moveable apart from plants, or fixed. This Latin word also means "human," a specific being of the animal world. A combining form of the word *homo* appearing in loanwords from Greek means "same."

After God had created every kind of animal that would walk, run, fly, crawl, or swim, we read, "...male and female created he them" (Genesis 1:27). God made the increase and continuance of the animal world a co–sexual partnership. The male has to fertilize the egg of the female in order for the species to exist in the future. Also, for example, it takes both the male and the female bird to build a nest, hatch the eggs, and feed the new little birds until they are strong enough to take care of themselves. Satan is always in evidence to pervert or change God's will for the world and mankind, and the male and female relationship within the human species is where he has always done some of the most abominable, evil, and perverted work.

As related in the previous chapter, it is evident that before the flood, men became sexually active with men, and women with women.

For this cause God gave them up unto vile affections: for even their women did change the natural use into that which is against nature: And likewise also the men, leaving the natural use of the woman, burned in their lust one toward another; men with men working that which is unseemly, and receiving in themselves that recompence of their error which was meet.

—Romans 1:26–27

A homosexual is one who desires or uncontrollably craves to have sex with members of his or her own sex. We note the word "burning" in Paul's description. Homosexuals have been documented as engaging in sexual behavior with hundreds, one of the main reasons for the worldwide spread of the pandemic disease AIDS. As indicated in Paul's referencing of God's condemnation of this sin, such people descend to a lower moral level than animals, and they are so demonically possessed that, as He did at Sodom and Gomorrah, God gives them up when they will not repent. There is reason to believe that the citizens of Sodom and Gomorrah were also infected with AIDS, and God removed this blight to keep the entire human world from being infected. The same could also apply to the generation of mankind that lived before the great flood.

The following appeared in "The Gay Manifesto" website, was entered in the *Congressional Record*, and noted in Dr. James Dobson's book *Bringing Up Boys.* It is being claimed by the homosexual lobby that this item was not intended to be taken seriously, as it was "only an essay." But this so-called "essay" that was first published in *Gay Community News,* February 15, 1987, has been aggressively promoted, and much already fulfilled, on the local, state, national, and international levels:

This essay is an outré, madness, a tragic, cruel fantasy, an eruption of inner rage, on how the oppressed desperately dream of being the oppressor.

We shall sodomize your sons, emblems of your feeble masculinity, of your shallow dreams and vulgar lies. We shall seduce them in your schools, in your dormitories, in your gymnasiums, in your locker rooms, in your sports arenas, in your seminaries, in your youth groups, in your movie theater bathrooms, in your army bunkhouses, in your truck stops, in your all male clubs, in your houses of Congress, wherever men are with men together. Your sons shall become our minions and do our bidding. They will be recast in our image. They will come to crave and adore us. . . .

All laws banning homosexual activity will be revoked. Instead, legislation shall be passed which engenders love between men.

All homosexuals must stand together as brothers; we must be united artistically, philosophically, socially, politically and financially. We will triumph only when we present a common face to the vicious heterosexual enemy.

If you dare to cry faggot, fairy, queer, at us, we will stab you in your cowardly hearts and defile your dead, puny bodies. . . .

Our writers and artists will make love between men fashionable and de rigueur, and we will succeed because we are adept at setting styles. We will eliminate heterosexual liaisons through usage of the devices of wit and ridicule, devices which we are skilled in employing.

We will unmask the powerful homosexuals who masquerade as heterosexuals. You will be shocked and frightened when you find that your presidents and their sons, your industrialists, your senators, your mayors, your generals, your athletes, your film stars, your television personalities, your civic leaders, your priests are not the safe, familiar, bourgeois, heterosexual figures you assumed them to be. We are everywhere; we have infiltrated your ranks. Be careful when you speak of homosexuals because we are always among you; we may be sitting across the desk from you; we may be sleeping in the same bed with you.

There will be no compromises. We are not middle-class weaklings. Highly intelligent, we are the natural aristocrats of the human race, and steely-minded aristocrats never settle for less. Those who oppose us will be exiled.

We shall raise vast private armies, as Mishima did, to defeat you. We shall conquer the world because warriors inspired by and banded together by homosexual love and honor are invincible as were the ancient Greek soldiers.

The family unit—spawning ground of lies, betrayals, mediocrity, hypocrisy and violence—will be abolished. The family unit, which only dampens imagination and curbs free will, must be eliminated. . . .

All churches who condemn us will be closed. Our only gods are handsome young men. We adhere to a cult of beauty, moral and esthetic.

All that is ugly and vulgar and banal will be annihilated. Since we are alienated from middle–class heterosexual conventions, we are free to live our lives according to the dictates of the pure imagination. For us too much is not enough.

The exquisite society to emerge will be governed by an elite comprised of gay poets. One of the major requirements for a position of power in the new society of homoeroticism will be indulgence in the Greek passion. Any man contaminated with heterosexual lust will be automatically barred from a position of influence. All males who insist on remaining stupidly heterosexual will be tried in homosexual courts of justice and will become invisible men. . . .

We shall be victorious because we are fueled with the ferocious bitterness of the oppressed who have been forced to play seemingly bit parts in your dumb, heterosexual shows throughout the ages. We too are capable of firing guns and manning the barricades of the ultimate revolution.

Tremble, hetero swine, when we appear before you without our masks.

In 1990, President Bill Clinton opened the Armed Services branches of the military for homosexual inclusion under the "Don't Ask, Don't Tell" legislation. However, according to statistical reports on various news channels, over eleven thousand of the Don't Ask, Don't Tell enlistments were discharged after they began crawling into the beds of their fellow soldiers. In 2009, Barack Obama announced to the nation that part of his program was to pass a law allowing homosexuals to join the Armed Services without restrictions. Chaplains have let it be known that if this becomes law, they will submit their resignations.

In the 1980s and 1990s, books, newspapers, commentaries, and TV commentators joined in a campaign to destroy the reputation and credibility of anyone who dared to write or say anything negative about the homosexual lifestyle. From the book published in the 1980s by Kirk and Madsen (*After the Ball: How America Will Conquer Its Fear and Hatred of Gays in the '90s*), we read: **"At a later stage of the media campaign for gay rights it will be time to get tough with remaining opponents. To be blunt, they must be vilified. . . . The public must be shown images of ranting homophobes whose secondary traits and beliefs disgust middle America."**

On June 1, 2009, President Obama signed a presidential directive making the month of June, which is traditionally the month of brides,

"Homosexual Month." In this presidential directive, Obama praised homosexuals some seventeen times. Referencing just a few lines from the directive:

> I am PROUD to be the first president to appoint LGBT candidates to Senate–confirmed positions in the first 100 days of an administration. THESE INDIVIDUALS EMBODY THE BEST QUALITIES WE SEEK IN PUBLIC SERVICE.
>
> My administration has PARTNERED with the LGBT community to advance a wide range of initiatives. At the international level, I have joined efforts at the United Nations to decriminalize homosexuality around the world.... These measures include supporting hate crime laws, supporting civil unions [marriage],... ensuring adoption rights, and ending the existing "DON'T ASK, DON'T TELL" policy in a way that strengthens the armed forces and national security.
>
> This issue affects not only the LGBT community, but also our entire nation.... If we can work together to advance the principles upon which our nation was founded, everyone will benefit.

President Obama and Dr. Rick Warren in 2010 both criticized the Uganda Task Force Against Homosexuality for trying to protect children in Africa from being raped and given AIDS. In its response, the task force brought out that the United Nations was disseminating UNICEF literature in Africa promoting homosexuality. Also, as indicated, President Obama has appointed a large percentage of homosexuals to important positions in his administration, including in the Department of Education. He also indicated in his presidential order that anyone taking the biblical position on homosexuality could be prosecuted, and it is assumed this would include jail terms. In other words, I could be sent to jail possibly for writing this chapter.

But God will not be mocked (Galatians 6:7). God had the final say in the days of Noah, and only eight were saved. God also had the final say in the days of Lot, and only four were saved. Through the Bible, Sodom and Gomorrah are presented as warning examples that any nation that descends to this level will be destroyed (2 Peter 2:4–9).

> Likewise also as it was in the days of Lot; they did eat, they drank, they bought, they sold, they planted, they builded; But the same day that Lot went out of Sodom it rained fire and brimstone from heaven, and destroyed them all. Even thus shall it be in the day when the Son of man is revealed.
>
> —Luke 17:28–30

Sign Number 13

Breakup of the Home

God established three institutions for the social and spiritual benefit of the human race: home, government, and church.

If the plumbing leaks, we can call a plumber; if the lights go out, we can call an electrician; if the roof leaks, we can call a carpenter; but if the bricks crumble, nothing can be done. The home is the bricks upon which a nation is built. If they crumble, the nation falls.

Paul wrote of the last generation before the Tribulation in 2 Timothy 4:1–4:

> I charge thee therefore before God, and the Lord Jesus Christ, who shall judge the quick and the dead at his appearing and his kingdom; Preach the word; be instant in season, out of season; reprove, rebuke, exhort with all longsuffering and doctrine. For the time will come when they will not endure sound doctrine; but after their own lusts shall they heap to themselves teachers, having itching ears; And they shall turn away their ears from the truth, and shall be turned unto fables.

I can remember in the 1920s when we children at the time would never think of disputing anything our parents would say or command, and if we said one word out of place in school we would get ten swats across our bottoms with a paddle. I can also remember speaking in schools in Oklahoma and Texas in 1959 against Federal

Aid to Education, warning what would happen to our schools. In 1963 the federal government ruled that Bible reading and prayers in school were unconstitutional.

Consider what has happened to our nation since God was made unwelcome in public education. The following is from page 42 of Dr. Johnny Esposito's book *Temples of Darkness:*

> These are some of the horrendous increases since 1963 when we "expelled" God from school. Violent crimes up 995 percent; premarital sex for 15 year olds up 1,000 percent; premarital sex for 16–18 year olds up 300 percent; suicides up 300 percent; single parent families up 117 percent; unwed teen pregnancies up 553 percent under 15, and 300 percent for teens 16–18 years old; unmarried couples living together up 536 percent; sexually transmitted disease up 226 percent; divorce rates up 117 percent (would be more, but so many couples are living together); SAT average test scores down 80 points (970–980); unwed birth rates up 325 percent; teen (10–14 year olds) pregnancies up 553 percent; crimes against students up 3,000 percent. There are 100 murders on school campuses annually; 12,000 robberies on school campuses annually; 9,000 rapes on school campuses annually; 204,000 aggravated assaults on campuses annually; assaults on teachers have increased 7,000 percent; more than 110,000 teachers are attacked in our nations schools annually.

According to government statistics in the *2010 World Almanac,* in the last sixteen years 80 million babies have been born in the United States with more than that number being aborted. But of the 80 million born in the last sixteen years, 40 million have been born out of wedlock and raised in a one–parent home. At least half of this 40 million will, in due course, if not already, be arrested for a crime, with a large percentage ending up in jail before they are twenty–one years of age. Without help from God, the parents, teachers, or local, state, and federal laws cannot control the present younger generation. This is not to say that every young person today is included in these statistics, but the statistics speak for themselves, and this is exactly what the prophetic Word of God says would happen to the last generation.

> This know also, that in the last days perilous times shall come. For men shall be lovers of their own selves, covetous, boasters, proud, blasphemers, disobedient to parents, unthankful, unholy, Without natural affection, trucebreakers, false accusers, incontinent, fierce, despisers of those that are good, Traitors, heady,

highminded, lovers of pleasures more than lovers of God; Having a form of godliness, but denying the power thereof: from such turn away. For of this sort are they which creep into houses, and lead captive silly women laden with sins, led away with divers lusts, Ever learning, and never able to come to the knowledge of the truth. Now as Jannes and Jambres withstood Moses, so do these also resist the truth: men of corrupt minds, reprobate concerning the faith. But they shall proceed no further: for their folly shall be manifest unto all men, as theirs also was.

—2 Timothy 3:1–9

The Bible is explicit: a generation that will not control its youth will be destroyed in the next generation. In 1963 our schools were Number One in science and mathematics in all the world. Today, our schools are almost at the very bottom.

Paul said this would occur in the latter times, and this is just another sign to the present generation that these are indeed the last days and Jesus is coming soon, because there is a limit to God's patience with a rebellious people.

Sign Number 14

Apostasy in the Pulpits

The Apostle Paul in his last epistle to Timothy wrote:

> I charge thee therefore before God, and the Lord Jesus Christ, who shall judge the quick and the dead at his appearing and his kingdom; Preach the word; be instant in season, out of season; reprove, rebuke, exhort with all longsuffering and doctrine. For the time will come when they will not endure sound doctrine; but after their own lusts shall they heap to themselves teachers, having itching ears.
>
> —2 Timothy 4:1–3

Most so-called new versions of the Bible even omit the word "doctrine" from the text. And Peter warned about the apostasy that would consume many churches and denominations in the last days:

> But there were false prophets also among the people, even as there shall be false teachers among you, who privily shall bring in damnable heresies, even denying the Lord that bought them, and bring upon themselves swift destruction. And many shall follow their pernicious ways; by reason of whom the way of truth shall be evil spoken of.
>
> —2 Peter 2:1–2

Peter continued to warn that what happened to the people of Sodom and Gomorrah would also happen to the last generation. Jude exhorted Christians in the last days to beware of false prophets who would pervert the truth:

> Beloved, when I gave all diligence to write unto you of the common salvation, it was needful for me to write unto you, and exhort you that ye should earnestly contend for the faith which was once delivered unto the saints. For there are certain men crept in unawares, who were before of old ordained to this condemnation, ungodly men, turning the grace of our God into lasciviousness, and denying the only Lord God, and our Lord Jesus Christ. . . . Even as Sodom and Gomorrha, and the cities about them in like manner, giving themselves over to fornication, and going after strange flesh, are set forth for an example, suffering the vengeance of eternal fire. Likewise also these filthy dreamers defile the flesh, despise dominion, and speak evil of dignities.
>
> Jude 1:3–4,7–8.

On June 1, 2009, President Barack Obama signed a presidential order making June homosexual month and boasted that he had partnered with the "gays" and would appoint them to high positions in his administration, which he has. Why was there no mention of this even from the pulpits of churches around the world? The reason is provided by Joe Dallas in his book *The Gay Gospel:*

> . . . Pro-gay theology takes it a step farther by redefining homosexuality as being God-ordained and morally permissible:
>
>> "I have learned to accept and even celebrate my sexual orientation as another of God's good gifts."
>>
>> —Gay author Mel White
>
>> "How could we go on being ashamed of something that God created? Yes, God created homosexuals and homosexuality."
>>
>> —Reverend Troy Perry, founder, Metropolitan Community Church
>
>> "I offered thanks to God for the gift of being gay."
>>
>> —Gay priest Malcom Boyd

When God is alleged to sanction the abominable, a religious travesty is being played out, and boldly. The travesty is twofold. Not only are believers falling into homosexual sin and legitimizing it, but uninformed

heterosexual Christians are applauding them as they do! Prominent religious figures and Christian organizations are giving a friendly nod to gay ideology, making Isaiah's famous warning more relevant than ever: "Woe unto them that call evil good, and good evil; that put darkness for light, and light for darkness . . ." (Isaiah 5:20).

A Growing Movement

To get a sense of the prevalence of darkness being called light, even among professing Christians, consider just a few of the gains the pro-gay religious movement within the Christian church had made as of mid-2006:

» Four of America's most visible mainline Protestant denominations—the United Methodist Church, the Evangelical Lutheran Church of America, the Presbyterian Church USA, and the Episcopal Church—contain thriving pro-homosexual groups that tirelessly lobby their denomination to officially condone homosexual practices and ordain openly homosexual pastors.

» The Episcopal Church's House of Bishops voted in 2003 to confirm the Rev. Gene Robinson as the first openly homosexual Episcopalian bishop. Regardless of the distress and division the confirmation generated within the denomination, official Episcopal Church spokesman Daniel England hailed the confirmation as "an important step for the church."

» The son of radio teacher and pastor Chuck Smith, who is regarded as one of today's foremost Bible teachers and is founder of the widely respected Calvary Chapel church fellowship, has publicly declared he is no longer certain the Bible condemns homosexuality. "I need to investigate more thoroughly," said Chuck Smith Jr., pastor of Calvary Chapel Capistrano Beach in Southern California, when asked about biblical references to homosexuality. Departing radically from his father's orthodox views, Smith Jr. also condones gay adoption and affirms that "gay" and "Christian" aren't contradictory. "I know two young men who've been monogamous partners for seven years," he states. "They've adopted a son who's thriving, they're good people, they've asked Jesus into their hearts and seek to live Christian lives."

» An October 2000 episode of the popular television series "The West Wing" featured the president of the United States (a fictitious character named Bartlet) reciting a lengthy pro-gay interpretation of the Old Testament Levitical codes prohibiting homosexuality. The character is portrayed in a positive light as he humiliates a woman who still believes the Old Testament prohibits this behavior.

» Grammy Award–winning gospel singer Cynthia Clawson, a prominent figure in Christian music for decades, has become a regularly featured guest singer at gay churches and pro–gay events. When criticized for publicly aligning herself with churches that condone homosexuality, Clawson dismisses the subject as a non–issue, stating, "Jesus never said anything about gay people. How important could it have been to Him if He did not mention it?"

» Ken Medema, another popular gospel artist who frequently performs at conservative Christian events and churches, is also a defender of the pro–gay religious movement. Though heterosexual, he endorses the notion that homosexuality is legitimate in God's sight and, like Clawson, lends his talents to meetings of "gay Christian" groups.

» Former president Jimmy Carter, when addressing a meeting of the Cooperative Baptist Fellowship, compared homosexuality to other secondary issues that "in God's eyes, fade into relative insignificance, as did circumcision in the first days of the early church."

» Brian McLaren, widely known as an author and leader within the Emergent Church movement, seems to share President Carter's ambiguity on the subject. In an interview with *Christianity Today's* online "Leadership Journal," he recounts his refusal to give a straight answer when asked where he stood on homosexuality.

"Many of us don't know what we should think about homosexuality. We've heard all sides but no position has yet own our confidence." In light of his (and supposedly many others') inability to decide what's right or wrong on the matter, he recommends a "five-year moratorium on making pronouncements," during which he suggests we "keep our ears attuned to scholars in biblical studies, theology, ethics, psychology, genetics, sociology, and related fields."

McLaren's words echo a common sentiment growing among people who claim the Bible is either vague when it comes to sexual ethics, or perhaps just needs a little help from the social sciences. While stopping short of saying "Homosexuality is okay," he and others suggest that Scripture is unclear on the matter and, to gain clarity, we need to consider not only what Paul and Moses had to say, but also what today's psychologists, sociologists, and philosophers think.

Adding to the problem are the denominations that, despite their official positions on homosexuality, are reconsidering the matter or allowing their members to ignore their stated policies on sexual conduct. A confused believer does not have to visit a "gay church," as I did, for affirmation of his homosexuality. Several Protestant bodies contain both leaders and parishioners who fully embrace the pro-gay position, even while their denominations technically reject it.

In 2009 the nation of Uganda passed laws to protect minor children from being raped and infected with AIDS, which is a sentence of death. Dr. Rick Warren, probably the most prominent and noted non-Catholic minister in the world, protested to the Pastoral Alliance in Uganda: "The freedom to make moral choices [heterosexual or homosexual sex] and to free expression [any type of sex] are gifts endowed by God. . . . I urge you, the pastors of Uganda, to speak out against this proposed law."

Forty times in the Old Testament God warned the nations about what happened to Sodom and Gomorrah. Seven times in the Gospels Jesus warned about Sodom and Gomorrah, and as we have previously noted, He said in the last generation it would be Sodom and Gomorrah all over again. The non-Christians may have an excuse, but certainly not ministers of the Gospel. This is a conscious rebellion against God.

In the early 1900s, a group of the most recognized Bible scholars, like Spurgeon, Bagelein, and others, observed that the falling away as evidenced in the ministerial ranks was in evidence. They set forth five doctrinal positions that would identify a fundamental minister of the Gospel. They were:

- » The inerrancy and full authority of the Bible
- » The virgin birth and full deity of Jesus Christ
- » The bodily resurrection of Jesus Christ from the dead
- » Christ's atoning, vicarious death for the sins of the world
- » The literal Second Coming of Jesus Christ

May 23, 2005, Dr. Rick Warren, was quoted by the *Philadelphia Inquirer* as saying before the Pew Forum on Religion, "Fundamentalists are the worst enemies we have in the 21st century," stating that the five fundamentals of the faith were narrow and legalistic. Dr. Warren boasts that he has trained over six hundred thousand ministers, all of whom will evidently believe just as he believes and teaches. The ministers at our ministry spend half their time some days counseling with brokenhearted church members whose churches have followed the Warren program of the Purpose Driven Church.

Dr. Rick Warren

Dr. Warren, or any of the pro–sodomite, anti–biblical ministers, will never dare reference the signs of the times or ever say anything about the Second Coming of Jesus Christ. They don't want Jesus to come back because they are building their own kingdom here on earth. Of them we read in 2 Peter 3:4–5:

> And saying, Where is the promise of his coming? for since the fathers fell asleep, all things continue as they were from the beginning of the creation. For this they willingly are ignorant of, that by the word of God the heavens were of old, and the earth standing out of the water and in the water.

Of these Peter said: "But these, as natural brute beasts, made to be taken and destroyed, speak evil of the things that they understand not; and shall utterly perish in their own corruption" (2 Peter 2:12).

Peter understood that Israel would suffer judgment because the nation had rejected its Messiah and that even the temple must be destroyed as Jesus had prophesied within the context of the Olivet Discourse. He also understood that those within the church who departed from the faith would also be destroyed in like manner.

> Ye therefore, beloved, seeing ye know these things before, beware lest

ye also, being led away with the error of the wicked, fall from your own stedfastness.

—2 Peter 3:17

The increasing apostasy within the organized churches and denominations indicates that the return of Jesus Christ must be near, even at the door.

SIGN NUMBER 15

POPULATIONS IN PROPHECY

In several preceding chapters we have alluded to the population on earth before and after the flood, as well as the increasing population of the nations in the last days. However, there are some prophecies in numerics that need to be addressed further.

As referenced in Josephus, it would appear the population of Israel at the time of the destruction of Jerusalem in A.D. 70 would have been approximately 3 million. The best figures available at the time of Jesus' earthly mission would indicate in A.D. 30 the population would have been around 2.8 million.

We read in the tenth chapter of Matthew that Jesus sent his twelve apostles into the cities of Israel, but they were not to go into the cities of Samaria. They were to declare the good news to the Jews that they were to repent, for the Kingdom of Heaven was at hand. Later in Luke 10 we read that He also sent seventy disciples throughout Israel, including the cities of Samaria. The seventy were to preach that "the Kingdom of Heaven is nigh."

As we have previously noted, the number four or any of its multiples indicates probationary

judgment. Seventy times 40,000 would be 2.8 million. The text of Luke 10 might indicate they were not to go into Capernaum, Bethsaida, or Chorazin, because these cities had already rejected Jesus Christ as the promised Messiah.

Next, we notice as Jesus sent the seventy out on their mission, He promised them that nothing could harm them, including serpents and scorpions. When they returned, they reported that even the devils were subject unto them.

Now we go into the coming Great Tribulation when the Antichrist will command that everyone in the world must take his mark and worship him as their god or suffer the deletion of their heads. God has never left the world without a witness, and the entire body of the church, all Christians, will have been taken out of the world (1 Thessalonians 4:13–18). So God again turns to Israel, because the Church Age will have ended. He sends out 144,000 Jewish witnesses, not just to Israel and the West Bank, but to every nation in the world. Now, how many does He call? 144,000. Was John just picking a number from the sand on a Patmos beach? No! He saw in the vision the angel of God sealing the 144,000 in their foreheads, and he heard the completed number, 144,000, not one more and not one less.

What did they preach, inasmuch as they would have been preaching to Gentiles? They preached salvation by faith in Jesus Christ and His shed blood for the forgiveness of all sin (Revelation 7:14).

How could they have escaped the death squads of Antichrist? We read that, like the earlier seventy disciples that Jesus sent out to Israel, even the deadly scorpions that Satan will unleash from the bottomless pit will not be able to harm them because they are protected by the seal of God (Revelation 9:3–4).

Now we come to their number, 144,000. Multiply 144,000 by 40,000 and it equals 5,760,000,000. We know there is at present in 2010 some 6,800,000,000 and possibly a few million more or less. However, we should remember that the Rapture has already occurred, even before the first seal is opened, and the sealing of the 144,000 comes after the sixth seal is opened. Of course, the seventh seal releases the seven trumpets, then seven vials, etc. But it appears the sixth seal will have been opened sometime just before the midway point of the Tribulation, or the end of the first three and a half years. Considering the number of Christians who will be taken out of this world at the Rapture, and the number already killed before the sealing of the 144,000, it is reasonable to assume, considering the signs of the times, that there will be 5,760,000,000 when the sealing of the 144,000 takes place. This is just another sign that we are in the last days of the last days.

Enclosed in this chapter is a population graph. This exponential curve should prove to anyone that the theory of evolution is just imagination and nothing more. If man has been evolving for millions or billions of years, there certainly would have been more than 90 million people in the world by the time of Jesus Christ. In spite of wars, famine, diseases, and natural catastrophes, the population is now over six hundred times what it was when Jesus was born. The graph does indicate that when Noah and his family came out of the ark in 2500 B.C., there would have been only a very few souls left alive.

On the graph there are some bumps in the exponential line because in 1939 a world war erupted. The United States had 16 million men and women in the Armed Services, and other nations had even more in their armies than our nation did. This would have affected the population growth rate for ten years or more. The passing of *Roe v. Wade* in 1973 has also affected the growth rate, although it has continued to increase.

Population History

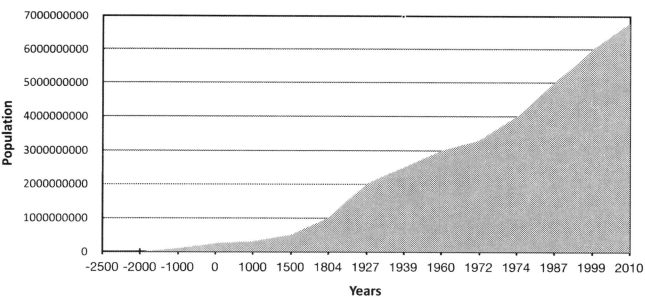

Sign Number 16

Radio

There are many things that this generation accepts as naturally part of our environment without realizing that just a few decades ago it was unheard of, or at least was an amazing miracle when it first appeared or was invented and developed.

One of these common entities today is radio. Most of the world's population today flip on their car radio without any more thought than taking a breath of air. When I was a boy back in the 1920s, radio was unheard of, at least on the farm where my family lived in Hugo, Oklahoma. We did have a Victrola that would play and produce music from round plastic discs. To us, then, that was a miracle.

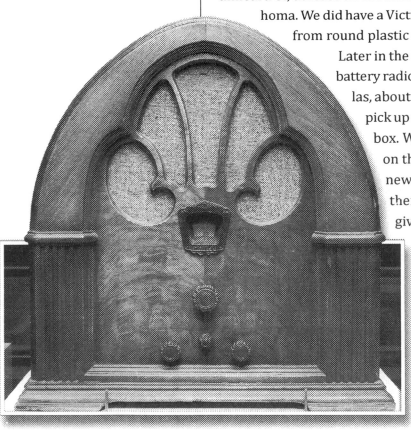

Later in the 1920s or early 1930s, my dad bought a battery radio, and out of the air, all the way from Dallas, about one hundred fifty miles away, we could pick up all kinds of music and news on this little box. We could hear Will Rogers commenting on the news, and we were fascinated about news of the Lindberg kidnapping case, and then we even heard about some woman giving birth to quintuplets. Amazing stuff. For the first time in the history of the world, sounds were almost instantly sent and received from a hundred or more miles away.

The beginning of radio seems to have been in 1885 when Thomas Edison applied at the U.S. Patent Office for sending electronic signals from one point to another. However, this process was mainly for wireless telegraph signals replacing the old system of sending electrical impulses by wire. Later, in 1893, Nikola Tesla was able to send discernible sounds that could be duplicated at the other end by use of a vacuum electronic tube. Then a Russian by the name of Alexander Stepanovich Popov developed the first integrated radio system. Another inventor that was involved in the development of radio stations and networks was Guglielmo Marconi. But radio as we know it today was not introduced into the United States until 1920.

Of course, there are radio stations all over the world today broadcasting thousands of different programming choices, including the Gospel of Jesus Christ. Anything that happens anywhere in the world that is newsworthy can be heard within minutes, or even seconds, at any other location in the world.

Jesus instructed those who would be looking for His coming again in Matthew 24:6: "And ye shall hear of wars and rumours of wars: see that ye be not troubled: for all these things must come to pass, but the end is not yet."

Before radio, television, and the telegraph, it might take months or even years for news to travel around the world. All the signs of His coming in the Olivet Discourse must be fulfilled in one generation, so radio has played in important part in the fulfillment of this prophecy.

Jesus also said in Matthew 24:14: "And this gospel of the kingdom shall be preached in all the world for a witness unto all nations; and then shall the end come."

Certainly, any individual living anywhere in the world can hear the Gospel over the radio. Also, satellites are circling the earth twenty–four hours a day broadcasting the Gospel to every nation. But I believe Jesus' prophecy particularly applies to the coming Tribulation. "And I saw another angel fly in the midst of heaven, having the everlasting gospel to preach unto them that dwell on the earth, and to every nation, and kindred, and tongue, and people" (Revelation 14:6).

One meaning for angel is messenger, and during the Tribulation even though every church is burned and every Christian either raptured or killed, and even the 144,000 Jewish witnesses silenced, the Gospel will still be proclaimed to every nation, perhaps by satellites. So the miracle of radio does have a prophetic role in end–time events.

Sign Number 17

Television

Perhaps no other contemporary invention has a greater prophetic role in the terminal generation than television. The capability to not only send sound over wire and space but also moving pictures developed almost simultaneously. In 1884 Paul Gottlieb Nipkow, a 23-year-old university student in Germany, patented the first electromagnetic television system. Transmitting and receiving systems were far more complicated than just sending and receiving sound, so the development of televisions for general public use was delayed. Radio, which was much easier and simpler to market commercially, was developed faster. The Great Depression of the thirties may have been one reason and World War Two another reason for diverting development of new scientific ideas to military rather than public use.

In World War Two in the South Pacific I was assigned a new unit for our 16-gun 90 mm anti-aircraft battalion. This was in 1943. This unit was a perfect radar system that could pick up a Japanese plane one hundred miles out, and by the time it got within shooting range, we could place a shell with the fuse set to explode within ten feet of the bomber. The new radar units were so perfect that the Japanese converted all their planes to kamikaze use. We could not shoot at kamikaze planes with 90 mms, so we were attached to the First Calvary Armored Division and I directed field artillery fire, using the 90s, for the remainder of the war. After World War Two ended, this newly discovered technology was directed to public benefit and by 1950 television sets with dinner plate–sized screens began to appear for consumer homes. Year by year screens became bigger, and in 1965 color programming was added. To local channels were added network programming from NBC, ABC, and CBS; and to network programming was added cable. Today, the average TV viewer has the option of a hundred channels or more.

By the year 2000 television programming had mostly re-placed newspapers, magazines, radio, and even the local church in providing entertainment, news, and even biblical teach-ings and in–house inspiration for those who found it no lon-ger necessary to get out of their chairs and leave their air–con-ditioned homes. While a small percentage of programming may be of informational or spiritual value, probably more than 90 percent is infomercials, Marxist indoctrination, reli-

gious hucksterism, meaningless and vain entertainment, and a waste of time that could be spent in more productive and meaningful endeavors. It is also true that of those who have taken up Moses' seat in telling the American public how to conduct their lives, what to buy, and what to believe concerning God and eternity, only eight out of one hundred have ever been inside a church. Therefore, at least 90 percent of the Ameri-can public are subjecting themselves to three or more hours a day of indoctrination by those who hold to an anti–Christian worldview. And pastors today wonder why their congregations are dwindling.

If we were to pinpoint one single entity that has brought this present generation to that moral and social condition of deterioration proph-esied in the Bible where men and women would be unholy, ungodly, lovers of pleasure more than lovers of God, and children disobedient to parents, it would be the advent of total television in at least 99 percent of homes today.

The following facts concerning television were found in an article on red–branch.com, a registered charity:

> Television watching reduces time available to participate in healthy
> activities and increases exposure to the marketing of unhealthy prod-

ucts. Children who watch a lot of TV have a greater risk for a range of health problems. Excessive TV watching has also been linked to poor academic performance. . . .

» 30 percent of national school students watch TV for more than three hours per day.
» In some national schools, more than 60 percent of students have a TV in their bedroom.
» In some secondary schools, 70 percent of students have a TV in their bedroom.
» In most schools (primary and secondary), well over 50 percent of students have a TV in their bedroom.
» One–fifth of secondary school students watch TV for more than three hours per day.

Scientific studies suggest:

» Heavy television watching is likely to affect performance in school.
» Adults who watch lots of TV tend to have an increased risk of type II diabetes and obesity.
» Watching lots of TV in mid–life has been linked to an increased risk of Alzheimer's disease.
» Heavy TV watching may affect children's cognitive development.
» Children with a TV in their bedroom do less well in academic tests.
» Regular exposure to bright light from television suppresses production of the key hormone melatonin. This suppression may cause early puberty in girls.
» TV viewing in childhood and adolescence is linked with poor educational achievement in later life.
» Children who watch lots of TV have a greater risk of becoming overweight, and children with a TV in their bedroom are at an even greater risk of this.
» Prolonged TV watching is associated with an increased risk of type II diabetes, and limiting TV and computer games in children may help to prevent type II diabetes.
» Girls who watch a lot of TV may be at an increased risk of getting an eating disorder.
» TV watching has been linked to risk factors for atherosclerosis and cardiovascular disease in adults.
» TV watching may result in daytime fatigue, with TV viewing in infants and toddlers being linked to irregular sleeping patterns.
» Adolescents and young adults who watch lots of TV have a greater

risk of sleep problems.

» Melatonin is a powerful antioxidant, and reduced levels of melatonin may increase the chance of mutations in cell DNA, which causes cancer.

» Slow metabolism—watching TV may slow the metabolism more than simply doing nothing.

There are also several important prophecies relating to the last generation that could not possibly have been fulfilled until the invention of television. We understand from Daniel, Jesus, and the Apostle John that the Antichrist will stand upon the Temple Mount showing his image to the whole world, and demanding that every person in the world worship him as God under the penalty of death for refusing to do so. It is obvious that people all over the world cannot go to Jerusalem to the Temple Mount for this occasion. But what you see on television is an image. When you see the president on television, you are only seeing his image. "And he had power to give life unto the image of the beast, that the image of the beast should both speak, and cause that as many as would not worship the image of the beast should be killed" (Revelation 13:15). A wooden, stone, or concrete image or idol cannot speak, but an image on television can speak.

Another time in the Great Tribulation when television will be in evidence is prophesied in Revelation 11:3,6–9:

And I will give power unto my two witnesses, and they shall prophesy a thousand two hundred and threescore days, clothed in sackcloth. . . . These have power to shut heaven, that it rain not in the days of their prophecy: and have power over waters to turn them to blood, and to smite the earth with all plagues, as often as they will. And when they shall have finished their testimony, the beast that ascendeth out of the bottomless pit shall make war against them, and shall overcome them, and kill them. And their dead bodies shall lie in the street of the great city, which spiritually is called Sodom and Egypt, where also our Lord was crucified. And they of the people and kindreds and tongues and nations shall see their dead bodies three days and an half, and shall not suffer their dead bodies to be put in graves.

This prophecy is explicit. People of every race, language, and nation will see the dead bodies of the two witnesses in Jerusalem. This could only be possible with contemporary television. There is a website that shows an area before the Western Wall at the Temple Site twenty–four hours a day. This could be where the bodies of the two witnesses will be placed after they are killed.

Jesus said that all the world would "hear" of "these things," and He also said that all the world could "see" these things that would come to pass (Matthew 24:15). This is just another sign that television is playing an important role in the fulfillment of Bible prophecy.

Television is one of the most obvious and important signs that this is the last generation on earth before the Lord Jesus Christ comes to be revealed to all nations, races, and languages, that He is indeed Lord of Lord, King of Kings, and the Savior of all who believe that He died for their sins and arose from the grave.

Sign Number 18

The Atom Bomb

One of the most fearful signs of the last days would be fear itself, according to the warning given by Jesus at the conclusion of the Olivet Discourse: "Men's hearts failing them for fear, and for looking after those things which are coming on the earth: for the powers of heaven shall be shaken. . . . And when these things begin to come to pass, then look up, and lift up your heads; for your redemption draweth nigh" (Luke 21:26,28).

I can well remember President Franklin D. Roosevelt in his fireside chats over the radio in 1932–33 encouraging the citizenry during the desperate days of the Great Depression. The president would close his talk to the nation with the promise: "The only thing we have to fear is fear itself." But that was before the dropping of the first atom bomb on Hiroshima in August 1945.

On the day that this moment in history occurred, I was at Clark Field on the island of Luzon in the Philippines. I had been directing field artillery for the First Cavalry Armored Division in the conclusive defeat of the remaining divisions of the Japanese army that had been driven northward to the northern half of Luzon. We had returned to central Luzon at Clark Field to await further orders, and we were wondering why we were not being readied to invade Japan, as it would be most difficult to carry out that kind of military operation in the winter. When the atomic bomb was dropped on Hiroshima, then we knew why. The emperor did not concede defeat at the dropping of the first atom bomb, evidently waiting to see if the U.S. had more than one. When the second bomb hit Nagasaki, Japan unconditionally surrendered. To us in the Army who had been fighting the Japanese, mosquitoes, the jungles, and bad food for several years, the end of the war was anticlimactic and bittersweet. It seemed as though the scientists had stolen the victory from us.

I remember from my high school science class that in 1936 there were rumors about splitting the atom, and even at that time there were efforts in Italy, Germany, and Switzerland to accomplish this. Dr. Albert Einstein was deeply involved in this project, with others like Dr. Enrico Fermi of Italy, and Dr. Otto Han and Dr. Lisa Meitner of Germany. It was Dr. Albert Switzer who wrote President Roosevelt a letter warning him that the atomic bomb could be in the grasp of Adolf Hitler, and this spurred the United States to begin the Manhattan Project that produced the first nuclear explosion.

Dr. Albert Einstein

Although Dr. Einstein was given credit for the mathematical equation that produced the atomic bomb, $E=MC^2$, he was actually not the one to calculate this initial key that unlocked the atom. This was introduced two hundred years earlier by one of Voltaire's mistresses, an extremely brilliant French woman by the name of Émilie du Châtelet. She was known at the time as the smartest man who ever lived, but was mistakenly born as a woman. She could speak four languages and discuss astronomy with the best scientists of the age by the time she was ten years old. Her algebraical commentary on Newton's *Principia Mathematica* is still recognized as one of the basic works on physics. Her husband, a French nobleman, allowed her wide open spaces in her affairs with other men like Richelieu and Voltaire, just two of many. She died in 1749 after the birth of her fourth child. While living with Voltaire, she studied the relationship of velocity, mass, and energy, and came up with the physics equation of $E_k = \frac{1}{2}mv^2$, which Einstein amended to $E=MC^2$ (energy equals mass times speed of light squared). However, few if any science books credit Émilie du Châtelet for the initial breakthrough for splitting the atom in the 1740s.

Émilie du Châtelet

As already noted, many scientists worked on this scientific effort in the late 1930s and early 1940s. There were several problems in heavy water experiments, which were finally solved by Dr. Lisa Meitner, a

Jewess scientist. Dr. Otto Han tried to take the credit, but it was actually Dr. Meitner who effected the breakthrough.

Although there have been no offensive nuclear weapons used since 1945, the potential stockpile that could be used by nations in the twinkle of an eye is frightening. No one really knows today whether we will be here tomorrow or not.

The nations that have nuclear weapons today, and how many, are as follows:

» **China**: 100–200 warheads
» **France:** approximately 350 strategic warheads
» **Russia:** 2,787 strategic warheads, approximately 2,000 operational tactical warheads, and approximately 8,000 stockpiled strategic and tactical warheads
» **United Kingdom:** less than 160 deployed strategic warheads
» **United States:** 2,126 strategic warheads, approximately 500 operational tactical weapons, and approximately 6,700 reserve strategic and tactical warheads
» **India:** up to 100 nuclear warheads
» **Israel:** between 75 and 200 nuclear warheads
» **Pakistan:** between 70 and 90 nuclear warheads

There are several other nations, such as Iran, North Korea, and Syria that are presently developing nuclear weapons, including megaton atomic bombs that could liquidate cities like Los Angeles and New York City within minutes. There is also the continuing threat of terrorists bringing suitcase bombs into cities like our nation's capitol and exploding them.

We have to count it a warning that man has never invented a weapon of war that he has not used. Even in our national anthem we read about "bombs bursting in air" and "the rockets red glare." The setting for these inspirational words was the war of 1812. At the writing of this chapter, our own president announced that even if foreign agents poisoned our water supplies or spread death-killing germs throughout our cities, we would not respond with nuclear weapons. He either knows something that we don't, or he is an idiot to put the lives of all Americans on the trading block.

We read in the book of Revelation about the coming Tribulation period that all the fresh water supplies of the world will be poisoned, all the green grass burned, along with one–third of the trees and millions of people being killed in one day. Such destruction and carnage would have to come from catastrophic weapons like atom and hydrogen bombs.

The hope of the world at that time is presented in Revelation 11:18: "And the nations were angry, and thy wrath is come, and the time of the dead, that they should be judged, and that thou shouldest give reward unto thy servants the prophets, and to the saints, and them that fear thy name, small and great; and shouldest destroy them which destroy the earth."

This is the **Blessed Hope** promised in Titus 4:13. Without this Hope, this present world would have no hope. As we consider that our very existence depends upon the good will and restraint of ungodly and vicious dictators, we know this is the last generation before the Lord returns.

> Watch ye therefore, and pray always, that ye may be accounted worthy
> to escape all these things that shall come to pass, and to stand before
> the Son of man.
>
> —Luke 21:36.

Sign Number 19

Liars and Delusions

The Apostle Paul wrote of Satan preparing the world to receive his own evil messiah, the Antichrist, in 2 Thessalonians 2:7–12:

> For the mystery of iniquity doth already work: only he who now letteth will let, until he be taken out of the way. And then shall that Wicked be revealed, whom the Lord shall consume with the spirit of his mouth, and shall destroy with the brightness of his coming: Even him, whose coming is after the working of Satan with all power and signs and lying wonders, And with all deceivableness of unrighteousness in them that perish; because they received not the love of the truth, that they might be saved. And for this cause God shall send them strong delusion, that they should believe a lie: That they all might be damned who believed not the truth, but had pleasure in unrighteousness.

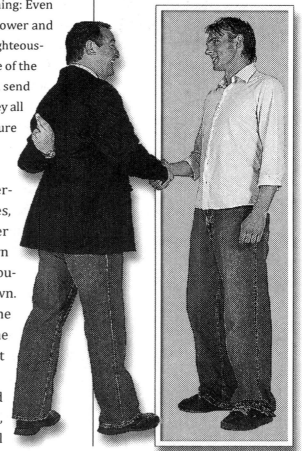

The world today, as we have already noted, has been literally immersed in the Gospel through churches, missionaries, Bibles, and Christian literature. Yet it appears that a smaller percentage is being saved than fifty years ago. The Southern Baptist Convention recently reported that although the population was increasing, that baptisms were alarmingly down. Therefore, Paul advised that in the last generation before the Lord returned, because the world at large was rejecting the True God, the masses would be allowed to be deluded, not able to discern between a lie and the truth.

We read in Hebrews 6:18 that it is "impossible for God to lie." This is why Jesus said, ". . . I am the way, the TRUTH, and the life . . ." (John 14:6). However, Jesus said the devil

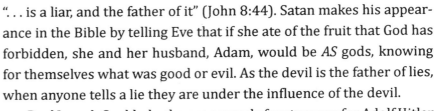

". . . is a liar, and the father of it" (John 8:44). Satan makes his appearance in the Bible by telling Eve that if she ate of the fruit that God has forbidden, she and her husband, Adam, would be *AS* gods, knowing for themselves what was good or evil. As the devil is the father of lies, when anyone tells a lie they are under the influence of the devil.

Paul Joseph Goebbels, the propaganda frontperson for Adolf Hitler and a violent anti–Semitic responsible for the methodical extermination of Jews in Germany, based his effectiveness on the proposition that the bigger the lie and the more often it was repeated, the greater the percentage of the masses who would believe it. By checking your concordance you can find literally scores of men in the Bible, including kings and supposedly godly men like David, who lied. Of course, in the course of events God judged them harshly for their lies. Some of the most reported liars of our time have been in the news media, like James Fray, Stephen Glass, Jayson Blair, Janet Cooke, and Jack Kelly. Sooner or later all the preceding were caught in their lies and were fired or had to return prizes they had "earned." In the political arena there would be, of course, Stalin, Hitler, Mussolini, Mao, Castro, Ahmadinejad, Arafat, etc. And who cannot remember President Bill Clinton on nationwide television firmly gritting his teeth and shouting, "I did not have sexual relations with that woman." He was impeached for lying. Richard Nixon resigned before he was impeached for lying. On the Internet there is a list of lies by Yasser Arafat against Israel that covers four pages—too many to even list, yet the news media in the United States have reported these lies as truth.

In recent years local, national, and international politicians have formulated a new standard for truth that is now accepted as the worldview of credibility. If a stated policy or fact (true or false) is accepted to be good for the environment, economy, or the military or political security, or betterment of the world, whether real or fantasy, then that idea, statement, or fact as stated, is promoted by governments and the news media as the truth standard. If a lie advances a cause supposedly good for people, then that lie becomes truth.

The United Nations came up with the idea in order to present a common enemy of mankind, a cause in which peoples of all races, nations, languages, and different political beliefs would unite to fight. This common enemy would present an imminent danger and energize the entire population of the world to sacrifice freedom, money, and property to attack it. Quoting from *The First Global Revolution:*

> In searching for a common enemy against whom we can unite, we
> came up with the idea that pollution, the threat of global warming,

water shortages, famine, and the like, would fit the bill . . . a common threat which must be confronted by everyone together.

This was decided at the U.N. Conference on Environment and Development in Brazil, 1992, and the report issued by the Club of Rome in 1993. While President Bush was not gullible enough to swallow this scam, the Clintons did, and this lie became a platform for the Democratic Party. The scam was that the earth was warming so rapidly that the ice in the Arctic Ocean would melt and cities like Houston, Los Angeles, and San Francisco would be submerged under fifty feet of water. All the ice at the poles is simply frozen seawater. You can put an ice cube in a glass and mark the level of the water, and when the ice cube melts, the level is the same. If the ice

at the poles would melt, it would be a good thing. In the Middle Ages, Greenland was green, which is why it was called Greenland in the first place. Temperatures were much higher then than now. You can check the high and low temperatures for the fifty states for the past hundred years and you will find that the majority of high temperatures occurred before 1950, and the majority of low temperatures came after 1950.

Are the ice caps really melting because of global warming, or is this another lie meant to confuse and control us?

Barack Obama gobbled up the so-called global warming scam as a major platform and political cause, with a stern and warning countenance telling the American people over television that they must elect him to put in a CO2 cap-and-trade policy or we would all be doomed. In the first place, there is no global warming, and in the second place, no heat comes from CO2—zilch, zip, nothing. Heat comes from the sun, and the fusion atomic process on the sun varies in different years; some years are hotter than others, some years are colder than others. CO2 is a vital

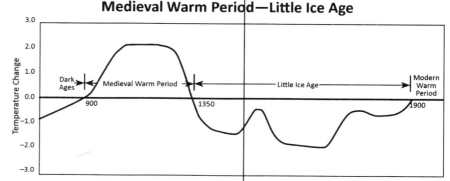

gas. Plants take in CO2 and make foliage, fruit, nuts, and vegetables. The more CO2, the more food we have. In place of the CO2 the plants take out of the atmosphere, they put back in oxygen. We breathe in the oxygen and give the plants back their needed CO2. CO2 comprises only from 280 to 385 parts per million, and 97 percent of that comes from the ocean. Of the remaining 3 percent, 2 percent comes from decay and non-human animal activity. A recent scientific study at Harvard concluded that we really need to increase that percentage to at least 1,000 parts per million, or increase it by at least four times what we have now. Instead, the Obama administration is spending millions of dollars trying to pump CO_2 back into the oceans and building huge windmill complexes that have to be sustained by taxpayer money. In addition, there are plans to install smart meters to control our usage of energy, even though they won't let the states develop new oil wells or coal mines with enough energy to last us for thousands of years.

Over 31,000 scientists have signed a petition documenting that "global warming" is a scam. The International Geological Association says it is not only a scam, but also insanity. They bring out that if CO_2 (carbon dioxide) was poisonous, all the theaters and sports stadiums would have to be closed down. One of our trustees, Dr. Edward Blick, who was an Air Force weatherman and a scientist at the University of Oklahoma for forty years, has written two books proving it to be a lie for political purposes. He writes that if we could increase CO_2 by just 1 percent, there would be an 8 percent increase in fruits, vegetables, and nuts. Unfortunately, the global warming liars confuse people into thinking that CO_2 is carbon *monoxide.* Dr. Blick concludes his book titled *The Global Warming Myth* with the following statement:

> United Nations politicians, while admitting their lack of evidence, gave birth and nurtured the fraud of *Anthropogenic Global Warming.* Their purpose is to frighten people into accepting the U.N. as the "centerpiece of democratic global governance" and let the U.N. ration our fossil fuel. In this volume, their data is exposed as false. That CO_2 affects weather or climate is scientifically impossible. We need more, not less. God rules the climate, not man.

It is amazing that in this enlightened and scientific age that the majority would believe this seemingly unbelievable lie. This is why the world is going to accept the Antichrist, who will appear on world television, "... whose coming is after the working of Satan with all power and signs and LYING wonders" (2 Thessalonians 2:9).

The Antichrist could be in the world today, and this must be the last generation before the Lord returns.

Sign Number 20

The Gog and Magog Conspiracy

The prophet Ezekiel was among the captives of Israel taken to Babylon after 586 B.C. when the city of Jerusalem was destroyed by the invading Babylonian army. Both Daniel and Ezekiel prayed to God for information concerning His will for the future of Israel, and the time that would lead to His fulfilling all His promises to Abraham, Isaac, and Jacob.

God revealed to Ezekiel that there would be in the time when the Kingdom promised would be near that Israel would ". . . in the latter years . . . come into the land that is brought back from the sword, and is gathered out of many people . . ." (Ezekiel 38:8). As I have stressed in this presentation of signs of the last generation, Israel has been gathered from many nations and is back in the land. As also declared by the prophet, the land was desolate and "waste," but as soon as the Jews returned, it became like a garden. After leading fifty–three Bible tours to Israel since 1950, I can personally attest to this.

It could be argued that the nation of Israel is not at peace in unwalled villages as Ezekiel prophesied. Of course, the cities today in Israel do not have walls around them, except perhaps East Jerusalem, because walls are little protection against missiles and atomic bombs. But considering what happened to the Jews in World War Two, and the wars of 1945, 1955, 1967, 1973, and 1983, I suppose

it could be said that in spite of continuing minor wars, that Israel today is in an era of relative peace. This "peace" in Israel referenced by Ezekiel could refer to a brief period after the Antichrist concludes a false seven-year treaty with Israel. There are also some who reference Ezekiel's description of the battle in which horses and bows and arrows are mentioned as the principal weapons, but no place in the Bible can you find futuristic wars in the latter years using planes, tanks, missiles, and atomic bombs. Had the prophets described such implements of war, the Bible would have been discarded centuries ago as the writings of mad men. We do see evidence of such weapons, as we have already noted, in the water supplies of the world being poisoned, the surface of the world scorched with fire, and millions being killed at once. The arrows that Ezekiel saw could be understood to be nuclear missiles.

The primary conspirator behind the invasion of Israel in the latter years is Gog, from the land of Magog. There have been books written on this one verse (Ezekiel 38:2), but perhaps none give a more simple yet adequate interpretation than the footnote in the *Scofield Study Bible* (p. 883).

That the primary reference is to the northern (European) powers, headed up by Russia, all agree. The whole passage should be read in connection with Zech. 12.1-4; 14.1-9; Mt. 24.14-13; Rev. 14.14-20; 19.17-21. "Gog" is the prince, "Magog," his land. The reference to Meshech and Tubal (Moscow and Tobolsk) is a clear mark of identification. Russia and the northern powers have been the latest persecutors of dispersed Israel, and it is congruous both with divine justice and with the covenants (e.g. Gen. 15.18, *note*; Deut. 30.3, *note*) that destruction should fall at the climax of the last mad attempt to exterminate the remnant of Israel in Jerusalem. The whole prophecy belongs to the yet future "day of Jehovah" (Isa. 2.10-22; Rev. 19.11-21), and to the Battle of Armageddon (Rev. 16.14; 19.19, *note*), but includes also the final revolt of the nations at the close of the kingdom-age (Rev. 20.7-9).

The attempt by Russia to incorporate the Arab and Muslim nations into its economical and political scope and purpose is historic. In 1978 when I led a Bible tour to Israel, Egypt, Jordan, Syria, Lebanon, and Iraq, the presence of Russian military advisors and armored vehicles were in evidence everywhere we went. Russia, this past year, invaded Georgia to keep the gateway open for a possible future invasion into the Middle East and Israel. Russia continues to maintain close ties with Iran (former Persia) by supplying needed technology for the development of nuclear weapons, which Ahmadinejad of Iran says will erase Israel from the map.

Aligned with Gog, the prince of Meshech and Tubal, from the nation of Magog, will be Persia, Libya, Ethiopia, Gomer, and Togarmah. On the sidelines will be Sheba, Dedan, and Tarshish (England, Australia, United States, Canada, South America, etc., would have been unknown and nonexistent as national powers in the B.C. world). However, this does not mean these nations will have a critical participation in this event when it occurs.

In Ezekiel's time Iran was Persia. Gomer would probably have been Germany, as one of Gomer's sons was Askenaz. Hitler sought to elevate the Aske-NAZ(I) race over all other races and eliminate the descendants of Shem and Ham. Another one of Gomer's sons was Togarmah, which would likely be Turkey. Turkey and Germany were allies in World War One. In the 1990s I led two or three Bible tours to Turkey, site of the seven churches of Revelation, the churches of Galatia and Cappadocia, as well as the mountain of Arafat. Turkey is a most beautiful country, with long mountain ranges with lush valleys and rivers in between. The army at that time was mostly pro-U.S. and joined in joint maneuvers with both Israel and the United States. However, in the background was also a strong anti-U.S./Israel, militant Muslim influence. With the continuing military presence of the United States in Afghanistan and Iraq, the revival of Russia as a growing military power with the invasion of Georgia without resistance from the West, and the refusal to allow Turkey membership in the European Union because of its death penalty stance, Turkey has again become aligned with the Russian and Muslim nations. Dr. Paul Williams, a noted educator, author, and columnist, noted this change in his column dated April 9, 2010:

> Turkey is now ruled by the Justice and Democratic Party (Adalet ve Kalkinma, AKP)—a party under the Gulen's control. Abdullah Gul, Turkey's first Islamist President, is a Gulen disciple along with Prime Minister Recep Tayyip Erdogan and Yusuf Ziya Ozcan, the head of Turkey's Council of Higher Education.
>
> Under the AKP, Turkey has transformed from a secular state into an Islamic country with 85,000 active mosques—one for every 350 citizens—the highest number per capita in the world, 90,000 imams, more imams than teachers and physicians—and thousands of state-

run Islamic schools.

Despite the rhetoric of European Union accession, Turkey has transferred its alliance from Europe and the United States to Russia and Iran. It has moved toward friendship with Hamas, Hezbollah, and Syria and created a pervasive anti-Christian, anti-Jewish, and anti-America animus throughout the populace.

In Ezekiel's day, Ethiopia included the southern half of Egypt, Sudan, Somalia, and present-day Ethiopia. Libya today is certainly one of the virulently anti-Israel, anti-U.S. nations in the world and would join any enemy against Israel. Two of the sons of Japheth were Tubal and Meshech, possibly twins. I agree with Dr. Pentecost that Meshech is Moscow, or the western half of Russia, and Tubal is Tobolsk, the eastern half of Russia, and both together comprise the land of Magog.

The ones who might protest but do nothing will be Sheba, Dedan, Tarshish, and the young lions. Sheba is probably Saudi Arabia and Yemen; Dedan, a grandson of Cush, doubtless means the rest of Africa. The best evidence is that Tarshish is the European Union; and the young lions, former colonies of Great Britain, including Canada, Australia, and the United States. Ezekiel 39:18 indicates this huge army of Gog and all his allies will come across the Golan Heights (Bashan) and there they will all be destroyed by fire, which could only mean nuclear weapons, weapons of which Israel has plenty in store. Ezekiel 39:3 indicates that Gog's arrows (missiles) will malfunction. Israel may have developed a secret weapon to destroy Gog's missiles in the air before they explode, or electronically cause them to misfire. In any event, fire and a rain of "great" hailstones will destroy the invaders.

Three places in Revelation relating to judgments of the Great Tribulation state that "great" hailstones will also fall (Revelation 8:7; 11:19; 16:21), some weighing up to one hundred pounds. I remember news reports covering the atomic tests in the Pacific islands after World War Two related that hailstones falling out of the atomic clouds were so large they tented the armor plating of ships being used in the tests. This is added evidence that the fire that will be rained down on Gog's armies will be of a nuclear nature.

As we consider Israel today without a friend in the world now that our present administration seems to be turning its back on this tiny nation in favor of the Muslim world and with the nations in their proper positions and alignments, the events described could occur at any time. They may not occur until the Tribulation period, but they could occur before the church is raptured.

While this opinion may contain some conclusions, nevertheless, these conclusions are based on credible evidence before us. All this constitutes another remarkable sign that this is indeed the very last generation before the Lord returns.

Sign Number 21

False Christs and False Prophets

The most important sign given to the last generation concerning the soon coming of Jesus Christ that will, of course, be preceded by seven years of great tribulation, is the return of the Jews to their ancient homeland and the refounding of Israel as a nation. However, perhaps the second most important sign given to the last generation is the rise of false christs and false prophets. Jesus mentioned the increase in pandemic diseases, earthquakes, famines, and other general end-time signs only once. Of the rise of false christs and false prophets, he warned three times:

For many shall come in my name, saying, I am Christ; and shall deceive many.

—Matthew 24:5

And many false prophets shall rise, and shall deceive many.

—Matthew 24:11

Then if any man shall say unto you, Lo, here is Christ, or there; believe it not. For there shall arise false Christs, and false prophets, and shall shew great signs and wonders; insomuch that, if it were possible, they shall deceive the very elect.

—Matthew 24:23–24

Concerning false christs and false prophets, false christs have to present a seemingly messianic plan, else they would not attract comprehensive if not unanimous adoration. The same is true of false prophets, even though if one of the prophecies of such a pretending seer does not come to pass, the Bible states that he or she is a false prophet. But this does not mean that all of the prophecies such a person makes are entirely false, or Satan could not use such deceivers for his purpose. It is admitted that some of the prophecies of Nostradamus came to pass. The prophecy of Malachi a thousand years ago that there would be only one more pope after the present one is certainly interesting. Many of the late Jeanne Dixon's prophecies were certainly false, but a few were interesting, like her prophecy that President Kennedy would be assassinated in Dallas, Texas. She missed the date by at least a year, but he was indeed killed in Dallas. She also prophesied that she was given a vision of a male child born on February 5, 1962, in the Middle East who would bring a new world religion and world peace after A.D. 2000. It was assumed she was foretelling the reign of the biblical Antichrist. In searching for a prominent world personality today who may have been born near that date, the closest we can come is President Obama, who was born on August 4, 1961, at Mombasa, Kenya, exactly six months earlier than the date for Dixon's prophesied world ruler (according to President Obama's grandmother in Kenya, and other relatives).

Of the false prophets on biblical subjects, who can forget Edgar Whisenant who in 1988 made world news by predicting eighty–eight reasons why Jesus Christ must come in 1988. False prophets on Christian television and news commentators and prognosticators today can be counted in the thousands. One of the most amazing revelations concerning the prophetic perspective of the general public was reported in a Harris poll dated April 13, 2010:

> » 57 percent of Republicans (32 percent overall) believe that Obama is a Muslim.
> » 45 percent of Republicans (25 percent overall) agree with the Birthers in their belief that Obama was "not born in the United States and so is not eligible to be president."
> » 38 percent of Republicans (20 percent overall) say that Obama is "doing many of the things that Hitler did."
> » Scariest of all, 24 percent of Republicans (14 percent overall) say that Obama "may be the Antichrist."

Quoting from the April 5, 2010, *Washington Times:*

NEW YORK | When FaithHouse Manhattan has its twice–monthly

interfaith gatherings, the guest list is a carnival of religious belief and creed. . . .

It involves unlikely alliances, such as when one of the most conservative Christian pro-life groups staged a news conference on Capitol Hill in September applauding a Muslim prayer service on the Mall.

It involves unlikely allies, such as leading Christian "emergent" leader Brian McLaren, who was roundly criticized during Ramadan last year when he fasted the entire month out of solidarity with Muslims.

It involves unlikely support, such as that offered by the Obama White House, which has identified interfaith work as a public policy goal. President Obama's Council on Faith-Based and Neighborhood Partnerships has an "interreligious dialogue and cooperation" task force that includes a female Hindu priest, an Orthodox Jewish layman, a female Muslim pollster, a nondenominational evangelical Christian pastor, a pastor and black civil rights leader, and a Muslim youth worker.

It benefits from some unlikely backing. Some of the biggest movers and shakers in the interfaith movement are governments in Muslim states: Jordan, Saudi Arabia and Kazakhstan. . . .

Evangelical Christians have been more resistant to interfaith dialogue but are slowly climbing on the bandwagon, especially with Muslims. Fuller Theological Seminary in Pasadena, Calif., has had three such evangelical Christian-Muslim dialogues. The last one, an April 2009 gathering, attracted 30 scholars.

We read in God's Word that the Antichrist will use the false prophet to cause all the world to worship him as their god. This means a world church headed by the greatest of all false christs. Dr. Rick Warren is acknowledged as the most important churchman in the world by the news media, and we quote him from the November 5, 2005, edition of *Time:*

Well, as I said, I could take you to villages that don't have a clinic, don't have. . . . But they've got a church. In fact, in many countries the only infrastructure that is there is religion. . . . What if in this 21st century we were able to network these churches providing the . . . manpower in local congregations. Let's just take my religion by itself. Christianity . . . The church is bigger than any government in the world. Then you add in *Muslims,* you add in *Hindus,* you add in all the different religions, and you use those *houses of worship* as distribution centers, not just for spiritual care but health care. What could be done? . . .

Government has a role and business has a role and churches, house of worship have a role. I think it's time to go to the moon, and I invite you to go with us.

Most Catholics consider their priests to be their mediator between them and God, but in the past ten years hundreds and possibly thousands of priests have been charged with sexually molesting children in their parishes. Even the present pope has been accused of protecting some of these pedophile priests.

A world news item dated February 19, 2010, reported that the government of China was highly offended by our U.S. State Department's acknowledging the Dalai Lama of Tibet as a messianic Buddhist deity.

In most so-called Christian seminaries today Jesus Christ is lowered to a religious leader who made some false prophecies about His coming back to bring in a Heavenly Kingdom. Other seminaries are graduating atheist ministers, those who really do not believe that Jesus Christ is the Son of God who died for our sins; therefore, they want a church and a ministry where they can help others "search for the real christ."

After the only church, that congregation of all born-again believers who will be taken out of the world at the Rapture (translation of Christians from earth to Heaven), those left behind can then decide the christ they want to worship, and that will be the Antichrist (Revelation 13).

The rise of multitudes of false cults, various religions, witchcraft, and occultist adherents all looking for that one individual who can save the world is one of the most evident signs that this is the last generation.

Sign Number 22

Signs in the Moon, Sun, and Stars

And God said, Let there be lights in the firmament of the heaven to divide the day from the night; and let them be for signs, and for seasons, and for days, and years.

—Genesis 1:14

We read in Psalm 19:1, "The heavens declare the glory of God…." Regardless how many theories that men come up with concerning the existence of billions or trillions of solar systems with billions or trillions of stars like our sun in each galaxy or star system, or how many "big bang theories" are proposed, no one can explain the heavens other than as biblically stated that an Almighty God created them. The only explanation the Bible gives for the creation of all these trillions of systems is to prove the existence of God.

Our own solar system is comprised of our sun, a medium–sized star, and nine planets, with a moon or moons around some of the planets. There is no evidence that life, intelligent or otherwise, exists on any planet other than earth. Our own sun, like all other stars, is a gigantic nuclear fusion (not fission) instrument that converts hydrogen to light and from the light comes heat. Our moon that revolves around our earth reflects light from the sun upon our earth. Therefore we can understand God had a purpose in creating our sun, our earth, and our moon, although it may be difficult to understand the purpose for the other eight planets, other than His Word that all the rest are to show forth God's glory and for "signs." We know that at one time, according to the Bible, the sun stood still, or it could have been that the earth stopped rotating, or at another time even rotated backward. What is difficult to comprehend is that as the earth rotates, we travel at 1,000 miles an hour; 100,000 miles an hour as our earth revolves around our sun; and approximately 1 million miles an hour as our entire galaxy rotates, making a complete cycle approximately every 26,000 years or so. Yet, we have no consciousness of moving at any speed in any direction. God indeed must be a marvelous engineer.

At times, some stars (suns) nova or supernova. A supernova is when a star develops a nuclear problem and explodes in an unfathomable nuclear burst that scatters flaming nuclear debris for millions of miles across the heavens. A nova is when a star goes out of atomic control, becomes hot and bright for a period of seven to fourteen days, the atoms are stripped of their shells, and the entire mass implodes into a ball only a few miles in diameter where the gravity is so intense no light can escape. Called a dark hole, there the heat is unimaginable and for eternity time would stop. Anyone would wait forever for the next second on the clock to tick. The "dark hole" corresponds to the biblical description of "Hell."

The fall of all the towers man has built will crumble at the time of the Battle of Armageddon and the return of the Lord (see chapter nine), and we read of a sign in our solar system that will just precede this glorious event in Isaiah 30:25–30:

> And there shall be upon every high mountain, and upon every high hill, rivers and streams of waters in the day of the great slaughter, when the towers fall. Moreover the light of the moon shall be as the light of the sun, and the light of the sun shall be sevenfold, as the light of seven days, in the day that the LORD bindeth up the breach of his people, and healeth the stroke of their wound. Behold, the name of the LORD cometh from far, burning with his anger, and the burden thereof is heavy: his lips are full of indignation, and his tongue as a devouring fire: And his breath, as an overflowing stream, shall reach to the midst of the neck, to sift the nations with the sieve of vanity: and there shall be a bridle in the jaws of the people, causing them to err. Ye shall have a song, as in the night when a holy solemnity is kept; and gladness of heart, as when one goeth with a pipe to come into the mountain of the LORD, to the mighty One of Israel. And the LORD shall cause his glorious voice to be heard, and shall shew the lighting down of his arm, with the indignation of his anger, and with the flame of a devouring fire, with scattering, and tempest, and hailstones.

At this time, God will heal the breach between Him and Israel that occurred at the crucifixion of Jesus Christ, as explained in this same chapter of Isaiah (Isaiah 30:8–13). As prophesied by Isaiah, the sun will be seven times brighter, indication of a nova, so naturally as the moon reflects the light of the sun, the moon will be as hot or bright as the sun on an average summer day. We cannot begin to imagine how high the temperature will climb on the earth. There will be real "global warming" and this could explain the burning up of all the grass and one-third of the trees in the Great Tribulation (Revelation 8:7). However, it appears this nuclear disturbance on the sun will be only a partial nova, because after the Great Tribulation the earth will become a peaceful and productive planet during the Kingdom Age. Following this period of extreme heat from the sun, it will go almost dark for a period of time, as indicated in Revelation 8:12.

This was confirmed by Jesus in Matthew 24:29–30:

> Immediately after the tribulation of those days shall the sun be darkened, and the moon shall not give her light, and the stars shall fall from heaven, and the powers of the heavens shall be shaken: And then shall appear the sign of the Son of man in heaven: and then shall all the tribes of the earth mourn, and they shall see the Son of man coming in the clouds of heaven with power and great glory.

Those who study the heavens, including eclipses of the sun and moon, consider these to be relevant signs concerning the soon coming of Jesus Christ. The September 23, 2008, edition of WorldNetDaily.com began with "Will Jesus Christ return to Earth in the year 2015?" This question was prompted by Hebrew scholar Mark Biltz. Quoting the article by World Net Daily:

> "God wants us to look at the biblical calendar," says Mark Biltz, pastor of El Shaddai Ministries in Bonney Lake, Wash. "The reason we need to be watching is [because] He will signal His appearance. But we have to know what to be watching as well. So we need to be watching the biblical holidays."
>
> . . . Thus, Biltz began focusing on the precise times of both solar and lunar eclipses, sometimes called "blood moons" since the moon often takes on a bloody color. He logged onto NASA's eclipse website which provides precision tracking of the celestial events.
>
> He noted a rare phenomenon of four consecutive total lunar eclipses, known as a tetrad.
>
> He says during this century, tetrads occur at least six times, but

what's interesting is that the only string of four consecutive blood moons that coincide with God's holy days of Passover in the spring and the autumn's Feast of Tabernacles (also called Succoth) occurs between 2014 and 2015 on today's Gregorian calendar.

. . . Biltz says, "You have the religious year beginning with the total solar eclipse, two weeks later a total lunar eclipse on Passover, and then the civil year beginning with the solar eclipse followed two weeks later by another total blood red moon on the Feast of Succoth all in 2015."

. . . Biltz was also asked about the famous statement in Matthew 24:36 when Jesus was discussing the signs of His "coming, and of the end of the world": "But of that day and hour knoweth no man, no, not the angels of heaven, but my Father only" (Matthew 24:36).

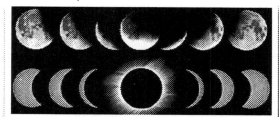

The Apostle Peter, the apostle to the circumcision, stated to the Jewish Christians in Acts 2:19–21:

And I will shew wonders in heaven above, and signs in the earth beneath; blood, and fire, and vapour of smoke: The sun shall be turned into darkness, and the moon into blood, before that great and notable day of the Lord come: And it shall come to pass, that whosoever shall call on the name of the Lord shall be saved.

The conclusion that Jesus may return in 2015 is an opinion and probably no more credible than the prophecy by Edgar Whisenant that Jesus would come in 1988. Nevertheless, it is interesting and to be considered with all the other signs in evidence today.

Even the most knowledgeable and experienced astronomers cannot assure that the earth will not be destroyed by a cosmic disaster. The *Economic Times* of March 12, 2010, published the following report:

LONDON: In what sounds like a chilling script of a Hollywood science fiction, scientists have claimed that an invisible star, five times the size of Jupiter, might be lurking near our solar system, occasionally kicking deadly comets towards the Earth

. . . They believe, the star nicknamed Nemesis or "The Death Star" could be hidden beyond the edge of our solar system and only emits infrared light.

In 1859 a solar storm on the sun was so powerful that fences and telegraph lines heated to red–hot and burned the prairies. But that was nothing compared to what is predicted for 2012. Quoting from *National Geographic,* December 20, 2008:

> An unexpected, thick layer of solar particles inside Earth's magnetic field suggests there are huge breaches in our planet's solar defenses, scientists said.
>
> These breaches indicate that during the next period of high solar activity, due to start in 2012, Earth will experience some of the worst solar storms seen in decades.
>
> Solar winds—charged particles from the sun—help create auroras, the brightly colored lights that sometimes appear above the Earth's poles.
>
> But the winds also trigger storms that can interfere with satellites' power sources, endanger spacewalkers, and even knock out power grids on Earth.
>
> "The sequence we're expecting . . . is just right to put particles in and energize them to create the biggest geomagnetic storms, the brightest auroras, the biggest disturbances in Earth's radiation belts," said David Sibeck, a space–weather expert at NASA's Goddard Space Flight Center in Maryland.
>
> "So if all of this is true, it could be that we're in for a tough time in the next 11 years."

Quoting also from InTheDays.com of April 13, 2010:

> IT IS midnight on 22 September 2012 and the skies above Manhattan are filled with a flickering curtain of colourful light. Few New Yorkers have seen the aurora this far south but their fascination is short-lived. Within a few seconds, electric bulbs dim and flicker, then become unusually bright for a fleeting moment. Then all the lights in the state go out. Within 90 seconds, the entire eastern half of the US is without power.
>
> . . . It sounds ridiculous. Surely the sun couldn't create so profound a disaster on Earth. Yet an extraordinary report funded by NASA and issued by the US National Academy of Sciences (NAS) in January this year claims it could do just that.
>
> . . . The projections of just how catastrophic make chilling reading. "We're moving closer and closer to the edge of a possible disaster," says Daniel Baker, a space weather expert based at the University of Colorado in Boulder, and chair of the NAS committee responsible for the report.
>
> . . . The most serious space weather event in history happened in

1859. It is known as the Carrington event, after the British amateur astronomer Richard Carrington, who was the first to note its cause: "two patches of intensely bright and white light" emanating from a large group of sunspots. The Carrington event comprised eight days of severe space weather.

There were eyewitness accounts of stunning auroras, even at equatorial latitudes. The world's telegraph networks experienced severe disruptions, and Victorian magnetometers were driven off the scale.

Though a solar outburst could conceivably be more powerful, "we haven't found an example of anything worse than a Carrington event", says James Green, head of NAS's planetary division and an expert on the events of 1859. "From a scientific perspective, that would be the one that we'd want to survive." However, the prognosis from the NAS analysis is that, thanks to our technological prowess, many of us may not.

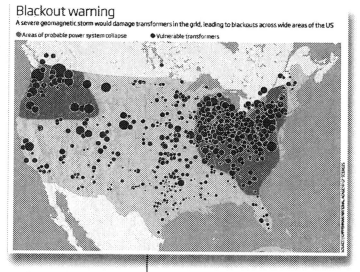

Blackout warning
A severe geomagnetic storm would damage transformers in the grid, leading to blackouts across wide areas of the US
◆ Areas of probable power system collapse   ◆ Vulnerable transformers

There are several dozen other scientific reports that could be referenced in this chapter concerning what could happen in 2011–2012 as a result of dangerous solar activity on the sun. We also should keep in mind that the Precession of the Equinoxes in our solar system occurs in 2012, an event that happens only every 26,000 years as our galaxy completes its cycle. No one that I have referenced or researched knows exactly how that will affect conditions on earth in 2012. It is well known that the Mayan calendar ends in 2012, as well as another ancient Chinese calendar.

Even if all these signs signal the nearness of the return of Jesus Christ, we know the seven–year Great Tribulation must come after the church has been translated (1 Thessalonians 4:13–18). Nevertheless, God has given us these signs so that we may know that we are indeed living in the last generation.

And when these things begin to come to pass, then look up, and lift up your heads; for your redemption draweth nigh.

—Luke 21:28

Sign Number 23

The Rise of Antichrists

As noted in chapter fourteen, Jesus gave as a dominant sign of the last generation the appearance of false prophets and false christs. The Apostle Paul in reference to the last generation warned, "But evil men and seducers shall wax worse and worse . . . " (2 Timothy 3:13). The Apostle John also advised, "Little children, it is the last time: and as ye have heard that antichrist shall come, . . . are there many antichrists; whereby we know that it is the last time" (1 John 2:18).

Many false christs, or antichrists, are to precede the appearance of the ultimate Antichrist, who will reveal himself on the Temple Mount showing himself as God to the entire world. People of all races, languages, and nations will worship his image. Also, as previously noted, this can only be done by worshipping his image on television.

There are several suggested lists of the most evil men who ever lived. Of course, we could go back into biblical history and perhaps include Nebuchadnezzar who destroyed Jerusalem and carried back thousands in captivity to Babylon. King Ahab of Israel would probably qualify as one of the most evil men in history. However, the Listverse.com list of the ten most evil men who ever lived is as follows:

1. Joseph Stalin, secretary of the Communist Party of Russia from 1922 to 1953. He is personally credited with condemning to death from 2.5 million to 10 million people. However, other reliable estimates indicate that those who died during his regime by firing squad, or in prison, would number between 80 million and 100 million. It is estimated that at least 15 million in the Ukraine alone died during

the communization of that region of Russia. After Stalin's death, others took his place until the Soviet Union imploded in 1989. A large percentage of those killed or who died in prison from 1917 to 1989 in Russia were Christians. I was personally involved in the distribution of some 15 million Bibles in Russia after 1989, and I never met anyone in Russia who had a Bible. In many ways Stalin was a strong predecessor to the Antichrist.

2. Adolf Hitler, Führer of Germany from 1933 to 1945, built one of the most effective and destructive war machines the world had ever known until that time. As will his successor, the Antichrist, he made a peace treaty with Chamberlain of Great Britain, promising "peace in our time," but broke the treaty a few months later. Also, as the Antichrist will do, his purpose was to kill every Jew in the world, and he is credited with killing at least 6 million Jews in Germany and Poland. World War Two, the result of his aggressions, resulted in the death of 35 million people. He died on April 30, 1945, committing suicide by taking a cyanide capsule and then shooting himself in the head.

3. Ivan IV of Russia (Ivan the Terrible) claimed the Number 3 spot on the list by his commanding that from five hundred to a thousand people a day be tortured and killed in front of him and his son in order to keep the peasants from rebelling. He is also credited with being the first tsar of Russia. Other tragic abuses and personal killings by his own two hands are too numerous to mention. Ivan's reign lasted from 1547 to 1584

4. Vlad II of Romania (Vlad the Impaler) had a reputation of entertaining himself in innovative ways by killing prisoners, enemies, people he did not like, or just for his own pleasure. He killed by tying limbs to horses, strangulation, impaling and watching his victims bleed to death, cutting off limbs, burning, sexual mutilation, etc. He was also called The Vampire. His reign of terror lasted from A.D. 1448 to 1476.

5. Pol Pot was the so-called leader of the Khmer Rouge. *Khmer* is the Cambodian race and *rouge* is red, meaning the red or communist peoples of Cambodia. Pot took advantage of the problems created by the Vietnam War in Cambodia to arm thousands of young Cambodians in their teens and twenties to take over towns, including the capitol of Phnom Penh. The cities were emptied, forcing everyone into the jungles and countryside. Anyone wearing eyeglasses or a wristwatch would be killed. All able-bodied Cambodians were forced to work in rice fields, also called "The Killing Fields." Pot is given "credit" for killing half of the 6 million population of Cambodia. His reign of terror ended in 1979 with the invasion of the Vietnamese

army. Southwest Radio Ministries hired twelve refugees of the Killing Fields, including my wife, Kim Ky. Seven of her brothers and sisters died in the Killing Fields, and one sister, along with her children, were buried alive. Her parents starved to death. I have had these employees of the ministry testify of the terrible slaughter, including suddenly splitting a worker open with a knife and eating their liver while they were still alive. Pol Pot died in prison in 1998, and it is reported that he accepted Jesus Christ as his Savior before he died. Paul said that if Jesus could save him, He could save anyone, but in Pol Pot's case, that would seem to be stretching the mercy and grace of God to its limits. We can only imagine if men like Pot can commit such things, what cruelty the Antichrist will commit upon those left to go through the Great Tribulation.

Others in the list of the most evil men who ever lived are: (6) Leopold II, king of Belgium (1865–1909), whose rubber policies resulted in the deaths of 3 million Congolese. (7) Idi Amin of Uganda (1971–1990), who during his years as president systematically executed at least five hundred thousand people according to estimates, as the exact number is unknown. (8) Ruholloh Khomeini, religious leader of Islam in Iran from 1979 to 1989. This mullah was in France and returned to Iran after the deposition of the Shah, a friend of the U.S. Khomeini was welcomed back from France, where he was in exile, by President Carter, with the commendation that he was a holy, charitable cleric. Once back in control, Khomeini ordered the hanging of all Jews in Iran and the killing of thirty thousand others who had been close to the Shah's government. (9) Maximilien Robespierre led the French Revolution, in which practically all of the aristocrats, including Marie Antoinette, and the Catholic clergy were sent to the guillotine. Some forty thousand others were also beheaded. Robespierre himself lost his head in 1794. (10) Attila the Hun, Sultan of the Hun Empire that stretched from the Danube to the Baltic Sea, ravaged Western Europe, which resulted in the breakup of the Roman Empire in about A.D. 475. He left nothing standing or living in his military advance. There are no estimates as to the millions he killed.

In this same list of the most evil men who ever lived, Emperor Hirohito is given honorable mention, or dishonorable mention, as the case may be. He, without cause, launched a sneak attack on the U.S. naval base at Pearl Harbor where not only the major portion of the U.S. Pacific Fleet was destroyed, but brought the entire Pacific area into World War Two, in which millions more were killed. The most savage act was the occupation of Nanking by the Japanese army in which his soldiers were given awards for killing one hundred or more Chinese civilians a day. Fatality figures indicate that some three hundred thousand citizens of Nanking were killed, women raped, and even children slaughtered. When I was in Nanking on one of our missions to China, I went to the main city office and the officials were impressed that I would ask for the records of the rape of Nanking by the Japanese army.

It is amazing, although not altogether surprising, that left out of this list of the world's most evil men is my nomination for the real Number One, Mao Tse-tung. It is not too surprising, though, because so many of the socialists, or communists, in the news media and even in our government, look upon Mao as a brother and comrade.

According to Mao's biography, readily available on the Internet, he was born in 1893. After grade school and high school in Hunan, he went to Peking University, where he also worked as a library assistant. At the university, according to his biography, he gravitated to intellectual radical and Marxists teachers. After returning to Hunan, he engaged in local political activities where he worked as a group (community) organizer. He founded the Chinese Communist Party and the membership quickly rose to over one million. Mao went to Moscow to further his education on how to follow Lenin and Stalin's examples. Upon his return, he was confronted by another young Chinese politician who had opposite views on China's political future, Chiang Kai-shek. Even as the Japanese armies roamed over China, the U.S. backed Chiang. Mao and his communist army waited the war out and finally won over the nationalists. As a result of the Mao communist program, the Great Leap Forward, between 1958 and 1961, 20 million died of starvation. In 1959, because of his failures, Mao decided to resign to the Kamindang. Premier Zhou Enlai convinced him that it was the capitalists, religionists, and counterrevolutionaries that were keeping his policies from succeeding. The two hatched a plan to publish his sayings in a *Little Red Book* and enlist millions of young Chinese, calling it the "Red Guard," to begin a campaign to cleanse the nation. As a result, according to conservative figures, 70 million were killed. In my missions to China after 1980, I never met anyone who did not have a family member killed during the Cultural Revolution between 1965 and 1975. Counting those he killed to become dictator, those who starved to death due to his economic policies, and those killed in the Cultural Revolution, Mao accounted for some 300 million deaths. Even so, the population of China today is 1.3 billion.

Mao—in my opinion—is the most evil man who ever lived, and I have to wonder as I pass his pickled body in the glass vacuum box on Tiananmen Square, if he might not come back to life as the Antichrist.

Beyond doubt, the coming Antichrist will be more wicked and evil than all of those listed so far in this chapter. He will stand upon the Temple Mount in Jerusalem claiming to be God. All who do not worship him as he appears on television, and willingly take his mark and his number, will be beheaded. The 144,000 Jewish evangelists will warn the nations that anyone who takes the Antichrist's mark and worships him as their god will be lost and suffer eternity in Hell.

The Apostle Paul called the Antichrist ". . . that man of sin, . . . the son of perdition" (2 Thessalonians 2:3). All who take his mark and number will go into eternal perdition (Revelation 14:9–10). It is no wonder that both Daniel and Jesus warned that this would be a time of trouble such as people on earth had never seen before and would never see again. It appears evident from many scriptures, including the fourth and fifth chapters of 1 Thessalonians, that Christians will be taken out of the world before this happens, just as God took Noah and his family away in an ark before the flood came, and Lot and his family were taken out of Sodom before it was destroyed (2 Peter 2:4–9). I believe this is the generation that will see the coming of the Lord, and every Christian should be witnessing to their unsaved loved ones and get them to the ark of safety that is in Christ Jesus before it is too late. The Antichrist may be alive in the world today. All the signs God is giving to this present generation as warnings seem to indicate that the man of sin is among us.

Sign Number 24

The Mark of the Beast

I was surprised a few days before writing this chapter to find an Internet item referring to the passing of a law in the Virginia State Congress to protect the citizens of Virginia from having to take the "mark of the Antichrist." I can well remember in 1935 the Franklin Roosevelt administration having to abandon a program called the National Recovery Administration (NRA). All those engaging in business or having employees had to have a national emblem of an eagle on their doors. There was so much opposition protesting that this could be the "mark of the beast" the program was withdrawn and portions restarted under other names.

The first noted mark put on a person was when God put one on Cain as a sign to others not to kill him for murdering his brother Abel (Genesis 4:15). Some believe the mark on Cain was the changing of his skin color, but, of course, that is a supposition rather than a fact of Scripture. The second reference is in Ezekiel 9:4,6 where the Lord commanded to put a mark on the foreheads of all who were in repentance over the backslidden condition of Israel, and then to kill all those who didn't have the mark. Whether this was a literal event or a visionary lesson to the prophet is open to interpretation. Under the Law, putting a mark or marks on any place of the body was forbidden (Leviticus 19:28). This would seem to make the placing of tattoos on the body an abomination. This is also one of the ways today that men and women get HIV, which becomes AIDS.

Placing a mark on a person, animal, or thing usually indicates ownership or possession. On farms and ranches in the West, especially in

open range areas, farmers or ranchers brand their cattle with a hot iron. Jim Jones would brand his cattle JJ, or the Bar X Ranch would brand cattle B–X, etc. The purpose would be, of course, to keep other farmers or ranchers from claiming their cattle. This same example would also apply to the mark the Antichrist will put on all who worship him as their god. All who have the mark will belong to him, and everyone who does not have his mark will be killed. However, before the mark of the Antichrist appears on the foreheads of his worshippers, God will first seal 144,000 Jewish witnesses in their foreheads. Now we are not told what this seal of God will be, but these sealed witnesses will be protected by this seal against the judgments of the Tribulation until their ministry has been completed, just as the seventy disciples of Jesus were protected as they were sent throughout Israel (Luke 10:19; Revelation 9:4).

The mark of the beast and the number of Antichrist are referenced in the following scriptures:

And he causeth all, both small and great, rich and poor, free and bond, to receive a mark in their right hand, or in their foreheads: And that no man might buy or sell, save he that had the mark, or the name of the beast, or the number of his name.

—Revelation 13:16–17

And the third angel followed them, saying with a loud voice, If any man worship the beast and his image, and receive his mark in his forehead, or in his hand, The same shall drink of the wine of the wrath of God, which is poured out without mixture into the cup of his indignation; and he shall be tormented with fire and brimstone in the presence of the holy angels, and in the presence of the Lamb.

—Revelation 14:9–10

And I saw another sign in heaven, great and marvellous, seven angels having the seven last plagues; for in them is filled up the wrath of God. And I saw as it were a sea of glass mingled with fire: and them that had gotten the victory over the beast, and over his image, and over his mark, and over the number of his name, stand on the sea of glass, having the harps of God.

—Revelation 15:1–2

And I heard a great voice out of the temple saying to the seven angels, Go your ways, and pour out the vials of the wrath of God upon the earth. And the first went, and poured out his vial upon the earth; and there fell a noisome and grievous sore upon the men which had the mark of the beast, and upon them which worshipped his image.

—Revelation 16:1–2

And the beast was taken, and with him the false prophet that wrought miracles before him, with which he deceived them that had received the mark of the beast, and them that worshipped his image. These both were cast alive into a lake of fire burning with brimstone.

—Revelation 19:20

And I saw thrones, and they sat upon them, and judgment was given unto them: and I saw the souls of them that were beheaded for the witness of Jesus, and for the word of God, and which had not worshipped the beast, neither his image, neither had received his mark upon their foreheads, or in their hands; and they lived and reigned with Christ a thousand years

—Revelation 20:4

Empires are identified as beast systems in the Bible. Nations become empires by becoming as predatory and carnivorous beasts eating up other nations: Britain—lion; Russia—bear; U.S.—carnivorous eagle, etc. Horns on the beasts are kings (Daniel 8:5). The last beast system empire will be composed of ten kings (Revelation 13:1), and the Antichrist will be a little horn that will be elevated over the ten who, with the false prophet as a lamb's horn, will enforce the "mark" of the beast system upon the world (Daniel 8:9; Revelation 13:11).

Regional national integrations like the European Union and NAFTA are transitional efforts to eventually produce a world government system, or as some call it, the New World Order. The *Financial Times* of England, November 2008, reporting on a meeting of the Bilderbergers, concluded that a "world government" was near. The Bilderbergers is a unit of the Council on Foreign Relations, with a membership of over four thousand top executives from the news media, political parties, banking interests, and even religious representations. The contemporary church of the U.S.A. is represented by Dr. Rick Warren. The late president of the CFR, David Rockefeller, boasted that the CFR would deliver the sovereignty of the U.S.A. to a world government. In December 2008, Henry Kissinger nominated President Obama to be the head of such a world government. That a universal beast system will eventually emerge out of the present world political confusion is certain according to Bible prophecy.

The king or dictator over this world beast system will be the Antichrist. The Geneva Reformers in the Geneva Bible of 1559 identified the Catholic Church as the Great Whore of Revelation and the pope as being the Antichrist. We would expect this, as the Reformers went to Geneva to escape being burned at the stake by the Catholic Church. There have been many who have used the numeric value of Greek or Roman letters to identify the pope or some other world figure as the Antichrist by adding up the value of the Greek or Roman letters in their names. Henry Kissinger was one back in the 1980s that was targeted by many to be the Antichrist. We are told the 666 number of Antichrist is the number of a man. Whether this is the number of a particular man, or that this will not be a government ordained by God, but by man himself, is debatable. Man was created on the sixth day, he has existed for six thousand years, his average height is six feet, and when he dies he is put in a six-foot-deep hole. I have noted that the popular Harris poll of April 2010 indicated that 15 percent of Americans think that President Barack Hussein Obama is the Antichrist. If we count the number of letters in his name, we come up with eighteen, which is the sum of 6 + 6 + 6. While our president does have certain identifying factors that suggest he could be a candidate for the office of Antichrist, we are certainly not saying that he is. However, the fact that there is more interest now in searching for a likely candidate indicates that the Antichrist might be alive and well.

In 1972 when the computer barcodes began to appear in markets on merchandise, magazines would depict people walking around with barcodes on their foreheads as either a sly or sarcastic reference to the mark of the beast. However, barcodes are becoming as outmoded as the horse and buggy. The new international identifying marketing item is the computer chip, refined to the RFID chip. And what is the difference between a barcode and an RFID? Quoting from an article by Scott Granneman from SecurityFocus.com:

Right now, you can buy a hammer, a pair of jeans, or a razor blade with anonymity. With RFID tags, that may be a thing of the past. Some manufacturers are planning to tag just the packaging, but others will also tag their products. There is no law requiring a label indicating that an RFID chip is in a product. Once you buy your RFID-tagged jeans at The Gap with RFID-tagged money, walk out of the store wearing RFID-tagged shoes, and get into your car with its RFID-tagged tires, you could be tracked anywhere you travel. Bar codes are usually scanned at the store, but not after purchase. But RFID transponders are, in many cases, forever part of the product, and designed to respond when they receive a signal. Imagine everything you own is "numbered, identified, catalogued, and tracked." Anonymity and privacy? Gone in a hailstorm of invisible communication, betrayed by your very property.

But let's not stop there. Others are talking about placing RFID tags into all sensitive or important documents: "It will be practical to put them not only in paper money, but in drivers' licenses, passports, stock certificates, manuscripts, university diplomas, medical degrees and licenses, birth certificates, and any other sort of document you can think of where authenticity is paramount." In other words, those documents you're required to have, that you can't live without, will be forever tagged.

Consider the human body as well. Applied Digital Solutions has designed an RFID tag—called the VeriChip—for people. Only 11 mm long, it is designed to go under the skin, where it can be read from four feet away. They sell it as a great way to keep track of children, Alzheimer's patients in danger of wandering, and anyone else with a medical disability, but it gives me the creeps. The possibilities are scary. In May, delegates to the Chinese Communist Party Congress were required to wear an RFID-equipped badge at all times so their movements could be tracked and recorded. Is there any doubt that, in a few years, those badges will be replaced by VeriChip–like devices?

. . . With RFID about to arrive in full force, don't be lulled at all. Major changes are coming, and not all of them will be positive. The law of unintended consequences is about to encounter surveillance devices smaller than the period at the end of this sentence.

RFID chips not much larger than a grain of salt can be inserted into any part of the body with a hypodermic needle, including the hand or the forehead. In a world government where no one can buy, sell, work, go to a doctor, or even buy an aspirin without an identification number, an RFID chip would be a necessity. This is probably why the new healthcare bill of President Obama will eventually—when it goes into full effect after 2012—make RFID identification a part of law. Quoting from an article on DailyPaul.com, "Microchipping included in Healthcare Bill?', August 30, 2009:

Buried deep within the over 1,000 pages of the massive US Health Care Bill in a "non-discussed" section titled: Subtitle C–11 Sec. 2521— National Medical Device Registry, and which states its purpose as:

"The Secretary shall establish a national medical device registry (in this subsection referred to as the 'registry') to facilitate analysis of postmarket safety and outcomes data on each device that—(A) is or has been used in or on a patient; and (B) is a class III device; or (ii) a class II device that is implantable."

In "real world speak", according to this report, this new law, when fully implemented, provides the framework for making the United States the first nation in the world to require each and every one of its citizens to have implanted in them a radio–frequency identification (RFID) microchip for the purpose of controlling who is, or isn't, allowed medical care in their country.

With our own president, by presidential order, making June sodomite month; appointing sodomites into his administration; the United Nations through UNICEF promoting sodomy worldwide; and hate crime legislation appearing in nations around the world, the laws of the Roman Empire after A.D. 70 may be reinstated. Then, a Christian had to renounce his faith in Jesus Christ, curse Jesus Christ, and then worship the gods of Rome. If the accused refused, then he or she was beheaded. This is what the Bible indicates will happen to anyone who refuses to worship the beast and take his mark in the Great Tribulation (Revelation 13:15; 20:4).

Are we really this near to the mark of the beast? The only answer is that we can now almost place daily headlines between the lines of Revelation 13, something that has never been possible before. Probably not one in one hundred church members are even aware the Great Tribulation may be just on the next page of our calendar, because their pastors are saying, "...Where is the promise of his coming?...all things continue as they were from the beginning of the creation" (2 Peter 3:4).

Part II
Irrefutable Signs of the Last Days in Israel

In this book on *40 Irrefutable Signs That This Is the Last Generation,* the prophetic signs relative to the nation of Israel are in a separate section so that the reader will be fully advised that Israel is indeed the most important sign to the world of the imminent return of the Lord.

The Bible says that "He came unto his own, and his own received him not" (John 1:11). Instead of receiving Him as the promised Messiah, His own crucified Him. In the last verse of Matthew 23, Jesus said to the Jews that they would not see Him again until they would say, ". . . Blessed is he that cometh in the name of the Lord."

It appears evident from the chronology of events related to His coming that the church (all Christians) will go to meet Him in the air (1 Thessalonians 4:13). Therefore, it is evident that Jesus is not coming back to this earth for the church. So why will Jesus Christ come back? Because God has made an everlasting covenant with Israel and the Messiah, a King of Kings from David, will dwell in their midst forever in the Kingdom promised to Abraham, Isaac, Jacob, and the prophets (Ezekiel 37:24–28, and hundreds of other scriptures).

I have led Bible tours to Israel on fifty-three occasions. The number of Jews in the land today who believe that Jesus Christ is Israel's Messiah is less than 1 percent. The Jews as a nation are certainly not ready to receive Jesus Christ with the greeting "Blessed is He who comes in the name of the Lord." There is not a town in Israel named after Jesus Christ. There is not even a street in Israel named after Jesus Christ. There is not a memorial, a building, or even a book in the library in Jerusalem about Jesus Christ, even though Jesus is the most famous Jew who ever lived. Today in Israel there is a 99 percent-plus rejection of Jesus Christ, even though millions of Christians from all over the world visit Israel daily and churches dot the land. Therefore, what will it take to prepare Israel for Christ's return to reign on David's throne for a thousand years (Revelation 20)?

What did it take for the Jews to return from Europe? Persecution! And, it is going to take the greatest time of persecution Israel, or the world, has ever gone through to make the Jews cry out for Him to come back—the Great Tribulation period of seven years.

The signs presented so far in this book relate to the coming Tribulation. The signs related to Israel are for the literal return of Jesus Christ.

"Behold, he cometh with clouds; and every eye shall see him, and they also which pierced him . . ." (Revelation 1:7).

Sign Number 25

The Diaspora

Moses prophesied that if Israel departed from the laws and covenants of God that a foreign nation with a strange language would come upon them. Their fields and orchards would be ravaged; their cities would be torn down; famine would grip the land and they would eat their own sons and daughters (Deuteronomy 28:1–62). The finality of this judgment is provided in graphic terminology in Deuteronomy 28:63–68:

> And it shall come to pass, that as the LORD rejoiced over you to do you good, and to multiply you; so the LORD will rejoice over you to destroy you, and to bring you to nought; and ye shall be plucked from off the land whither thou goest to possess it. And the LORD shall scatter thee among all people, from the one end of the earth even unto the other; and there thou shalt serve other gods, which neither thou nor thy fathers have known, even wood and stone. And among these nations shalt thou find no ease, neither shall the sole of thy foot have rest: but the LORD shall give thee there a trembling heart, and failing of eyes, and sorrow of mind: And thy life shall hang in doubt before thee; and thou shalt fear day and night, and shalt have none assurance of thy life: In the morning thou shalt say, Would God it were even! and at even thou shalt say, Would God it were morning! for the fear of thine heart wherewith thou shalt fear, and for the sight of thine eyes which thou shalt see.

Roman triumphal arch panel copy from Beth Hatefutsoth, showing spoils of Jerusalem temple

> And the LORD shall bring thee into Egypt again with ships, by the way whereof I spake unto thee, Thou shalt see it no more again: and there ye shall be sold unto your enemies for bondmen and bondwomen, and no man shall buy you.

In the Olivet Discourse in Matthew 24, Jesus prophesied that Jerusalem and the temple would be destroyed and the Jews scattered to the ends of the world. Forty years later in A.D. 70 what both Moses and Jesus foretold happened. The cities in Israel were destroyed and during the siege of Jerusalem, as Josephus recorded, parents ate their children; one million were killed; and the able–bodied who survived were taken to Egypt and sold on the slave market, which became so glutted no one would buy them. Thus began the age of Jewish dispersion into all nations, which is known as the Diaspora.

But Jesus indicated the dispersion of Israel would not last forever.

> For these be the days of vengeance, that all things which are written may be fulfilled. But woe unto them that are with child, and to them that give suck, in those days! for there shall be great distress in the land, and wrath upon this people. And they shall fall by the edge of the sword, and shall be led away captive into all nations: and Jerusalem shall be trodden down of the Gentiles, until the times of the Gentiles be fulfilled.
>
> —Luke 21:22–24

The Jews were to be scattered into all the world until the "times of the Gentiles" be fulfilled, or completed. Some believe the times of the

Gentiles began when Babylon invaded Israel and took control of Jerusalem and the temple, and will continue as long as the Gentile nations are in control of the world. Others believe, which I favor, that the period in which God's message of salvation by faith through grace is being extended to the Gentile world, or the Church Age, which began at Pentecost and will end with the Rapture of the church. The Jew is back in the land, but the Church Age is continuing and the gospel is still being preached to all nations. So the terminology of Scripture must mean that we are in the closing days of the times of the Gentiles, as Israel is being prepared for the future Kingdom Age. We have two ages interposing upon each other.

We have more insight to the depth and years of the Diaspora from the prophet Hosea:

> For the children of Israel shall abide many days without a king, and without a prince, and without a sacrifice, and without an image, and without an ephod, and without teraphim: Afterward shall the children of Israel return, and seek the LORD their God, and David their king; and shall fear the LORD and his goodness in the latter days.
>
> —Hosea 3:4–5

Historical evidence proves this prophecy. Israel was indeed without a country, a temple, and without a nation from A.D. 70 until 1948. It is also noted that they would be without a prince. We know what happened to the temple and the nation, but what happened to their prince?

> I will go and return to my place, till they acknowledge their offence, and seek my face: in their affliction they will seek me early. Come, and let us return unto the LORD: for he hath torn, and he will heal us; he hath smitten, and he will bind us up. After two days will he revive us: in the third day he will raise us up, and we shall live in his sight.
>
> —Hosea 5:15–6:2

The prince, or Messiah, returned to His place in Heaven with the Father because they crucified Him. Now when will the Jews learn they made a mistake? In their affliction! The word for affliction is *tsar,* which in other scriptures is interpreted "tribulation." In other words, Israel will not recognize their Messiah until the Great Tribulation. That is why the Great Tribulation period of seven years must come.

In the Tribulation the Jews who are still alive will doubtless be witnessed to by the 144,000 Jewish witnesses, and they will understand that the Lord has punished them for two thousand years for unbelief. One day is with the Lord as a thousand years (Psalm 90; 2 Peter 3:8). The Jews will then believe in Him as their Messiah and cry out to God to send Him back.

As we read in Revelation 19–20, Jesus Christ returns as the King of Kings, destroys the beast armies, casts the Antichrist and the false prophet into Hell, and reigns on the throne of David for a thousand years. Swords will be beaten into plowshares and there will be peace on earth for the entire Kingdom Age.

As Hosea prophesied, Israel was scattered into all the world for two thousand years for rejecting their Messiah, and in the time span of the last generation the Jews have returned and Israel is a sovereign nation again. Israel is surrounded by enemies and its only friend in the world, the United States, is uncertain. God has the Jews where He wants them, and the final act is about to begin.

God's Promises Concerning the Jews' Return

Lest there be some replacement theologians reading this book with any remaining doubts concerning why the Jew is back in the land, we present a comprehensive overview.

Jews arriving in Israel from Nazi–occupied Europe

The compilers of the Psalms, every major prophet, and a majority of the minor prophets foretold the return of the Jews from **all** nations as a prelude to the Messianic age. Some theologians, as we have noted, made the church Israel during the Dark Ages and the Middle Ages in order to try to explain why there was no nation of Israel. But James, the brother of Jesus according to the flesh, wrote:

> Be patient therefore, brethren, unto the coming of the Lord. Behold, the husbandman waiteth for the precious fruit of the earth, and hath long patience for it, until he receive the early and latter rain.
>
> —James 5:7

Many Christian scholars down through the centuries of the Church Age became impatient and presented the explanation that the church was going to bring in the Kingdom without Israel. Moses prophesied: ". . . then the LORD thy God . . . will return and gather thee from all the nations, whither the LORD thy God hath scattered thee" (Deuteronomy 30:3). Ezekiel prophesied:

> And I will bring you out from the people, and will gather you out of the countries wherein ye are scattered, with a mighty hand, and with a stretched out arm, and with fury poured out.
>
> —Ezekiel 20:34

Jesus prophesied:

NOAH W. HUTCHINGS 119

And they shall fall by the edge of the sword, and shall be led away captive into all nations: and Jerusalem shall be trodden down of the Gentiles, until the times of the Gentiles be fulfilled.

—Luke 21:24

Moses prophesied of Jacob and the descendants of his twelve sons: "As an eagle stirreth up her nest, fluttereth over her young, spreadeth abroad her wings, taketh them, beareth them on her wings" (Deuteronomy 32:11). While this scripture relating to the Lord's protection of His own can be claimed by Christians, it applies directly to Israel. An eagle, like most birds, will stir up the nest, throw out the feathers, and make it uncomfortable so that the young birds will learn to fly on their own. As Moses prophesied in Deuteronomy 28, during the Diaspora God has never allowed the Jews to become secure and comfortable. Books would be required to account the wanderings and persecutions of the Jews after the destruction of Jerusalem and the temple in A.D. 70.

Tens of thousands of Jews perished in the Roman siege of Jerusalem. Tens of thousands of the young and healthy were sold in the slave markets of Alexandria as Moses prophesied (Deuteronomy 28:68). According to Josephus, as many as five hundred Jews a day were crucified before the walls of Jerusalem to make the defenders of the city surrender. After A.D. 70 some Jews did remain in the land and others returned in the times between periods of persecutions. However, after the Bar Kochba rebellion in A.D. 132, a new era of Roman persecution began. Even so, in the sixth century, forty–three communities continued to exist in Israel (*Holy War for the Promised Land,* p. 56). One report indicates that even Mohammed led savage raids against Jewish settlements in the Negev. The Byzantines continued Jewish persecutions, and in the seventh century Muslims invaded Israel and erected a Muslim shrine on the Temple Mount. For the next thousand years Mongol armies, Muslim armies, the Crusaders from Europe, and finally Turkish armies waged wars over Israel with the remaining Jews caught in the middle. At the time Christopher Columbus sailed for America, the Spanish Inquisition, a time of intense Jewish persecution, was in progress. During the Middle Ages Jews changed their attire to that of the upper middle class in order to escape persecution. Today in Israel some of the orthodox still wear the black coats and hats even during the summer months, a leftover tradition from the Eastern European period of Jewish persecution.

In the 1930s a new era of Jewish persecution began in Germany. The March 15, 1933, edition of the *Palestine Post* carried the headline, "JEWS FLEE NAZIS' REIGN OF TERROR." The story continued to relate that the bodies of Jews in the Berlin canals were clogging the waterways. This was the beginning of the greatest era of Jewish genocide and persecution, **the Holocaust,** in which over 6 million Jewish men, women, and children were slaughtered.

The continual stirring up of the nest for almost two thousand years kept alive the Jewish longing for a return to their ancient homeland. In 1897 Theodor Herzl began a new movement for the restoration of the Jewish state which was finally realized in 1948. Some reports indicate that Jews have returned from one hundred twenty nations to Israel, but it is possible that today in Israel Jews may be found from every nation in the world, fulfilling the messianic prophecy that they would come back from **all nations.** This sign is, we believe, the most important messianic prophetic fulfillment.

Sign Number 26

How Did the Jews Return?

Some may wonder why Jews are referenced as Israelis, or Israelis are referenced as Jews. It was in the Babylonian captivity period that the Israelites were first called Jews because they came from the nation of Judah. While most who went into Babylonia were from either the tribes of Judah or Benjamin, there were Israelites from all twelve tribes. There is also a theory (referred to as British Israelism) that during the Assyrian captivity period all the members of the ten northern tribes were killed or went into other nations and became England, America, Denmark, etc. But even after the Assyrian captivity Israelites from all twelve tribes are mentioned in the Bible as being at the Passover in Jerusalem.

During the Babylonian captivity there was some mixing of the tribes, but even after they came back there are references to those Israelites who were members of one of the ten northern tribes. During the period of the Assyrian captivity, many escaped and came back to live in Judæa because they could not go back to the northern kingdom. Many of the Israelites of the northern kingdom continue to keep up with their tribal genealogy.

During the Babylonian captivity, because most were from the tribe of Judah, and all were from the nation of Judah, all Israelites began to be called Jews, regardless of their tribal genealogies. Even though we call all Israelites Jews, this does not mean that they are all from the tribe of Judah, although he or she could be.

George Washington, John Adams, and other founding fathers of our country expressed favorable concerns about the return of the Jews to their land. Napoleon even had a plan to join a Jewish remnant army in Lebanon and take back the land for the Jews. However, he made a tactical error at Acco and lost most of his army. God promises in His Word that the Jews would return after some two thousand years, but to what were they to return to? Were they to form an army and retake the land?

Theodor Herzl had fanned the fires of Zionist nationalism in the late nineteenth century, but the Ottoman Empire was still in control of the Trans–Jordan area. Perhaps with an ulterior motive, Great Britain, in 1903, offered the World Zionist Organization the country of Uganda for the establishing of a new Jewish nation. The appeal was that Uganda in central East Africa was a good land, about twice the land that was included in the old boundaries of Israel, and the Jews could have their own nation immediately. Nevertheless, the World Zionist Organization rejected the offer, citing scriptural reasons that Uganda was not the nation that God promised to the seed of Abraham. One of the scriptures referred to by the World Zionist Organization was a prophecy by Jeremiah:

Men shall buy fields for money, and subscribe evidences, and seal them, and take witnesses in the land of Benjamin, and in the places about Jerusalem, and in the cities of Judah, and in the cities of the mountains, and in the cities of the valley, and in the cities of the south: for I will cause their captivity to return, saith the LORD.

—Jeremiah 32:44

When the Jews began to return at about the turn of the twentieth century, they first settled in Tel Aviv. There were a few Jews who already owned homes and properties in other parts of what was then called Palestine, but

---

THE PALESTINE POST

Vol. IX No. 2379.   JERUSALEM, WEDNESDAY, MARCH 15, 1933   (Adar 17k, 5693 — Zu (a) 1 Qadeh 18, 1351)

JEWS FLEE NAZIS' REIGN OF TERROR
LONDON HEARS OF APPALLING PERSECUTIONS AND ANTI-JEWISH MEASURES

MAX REINHARDT FORCED TO FLEE

Berlin, Tuesday—London newspapers describing the appalling anti-Semitic Nazi reign of terror, declares that the bodies of Jews are daily recovered from the Spree, the Berlin canal.

Nazis in Koeln have ordered the immediate suspension of Jewish slaughter houses, confiscating all ritual appurtenances and driving Jewish butchers from the market.

Jacob Leshchinsky, who was arrested on Saturday, was released today and ordered to leave the country by Thursday.

Political police raided the Jewish Telegraphic Agency office here, finding nothing of an incriminating nature in an hour and a half search. Normal work has been resumed by the news agency.

Max Reinhardt, the famous theatrical producer, it is reported, has fled to Vienna.

Appeal to Polish Government

Warsaw, Tuesday—2,000 Polish Jews living in Saxony have requested the Polish Government to grant them passports, to enable them to leave Germany.

More than a hundred Leipzig Jews have already crossed the German border to enter Poland. So far, more than five hundred Polish Jewish families have reentered their native country.

Republican Flag Definitely Discarded

Berlin, Monday—The Republican black, red and gold flag has been discarded. The old Imperial black, white and red has been restored as national colours by a Presidential decree. This was announced by Herr Hitler by broadcast. The Swastika flag shares full equality with the Imperial flag and will be flown simultaneously on public buildings.

Herr Hitler described the flag order as "symbolic of the marriage of tradition and the young national revolution." He has commanded all public buildings in Germany to fly both flags for three days.

The Imperial Prussian flags were flying in Berlin on Sunday as a sign of mourning for Germany's war dead, memorial services for whom were held throughout Germany. President Hindenburg in the uniform of a Field-Marshal with Herr Hitler, and other Ministers took the salute of the Reichswehr, Steel Helmets and Nazi Storm Troopers after the memorial service in the Opera House of Berlin.

Nazi Chancellor Against Terrorism

Herr Hitler again has sternly warned his followers to refrain from terrorism. He says that the Nazi victory is so overwhelming that they "cannot stoop to take petty revenge." It was their task to restore a feeling of absolute security in the interests of the people, and especially for business. "Only when our enemies commit acts of violence will you be commissioned to smash resistance ruthlessly."

And "Unknowns" Shoot Down Solicitor

Herr Kiels Spiegel, a well known solicitor, who acted for the German Socialist party in countless political lawsuits was shot dead at his home at 2 a.m., on Sunday, by what the police describe as "unknown" assailants.

French Alarmed by Nazi Invasion of Demilitarised Zone

London, Monday—The Nazis' penetration into the demilitarised zone, which alarmed France, has been extended by the occupation of Speyer and Cologne where Nazi troops have taken possession of the Rathaus. The chief burgomaster, Herr Adenaurer, has been suspended by the Nazi Herr Riese.

land and space under their control was limited. So wealthy Jews, supported by outside Zionist contributions, began to buy land from the Turks, Arabs, and others who were willing to sell. The new city on the Mediterranean coast just east of Jaffa was named Tel Aviv, possibly a contemporary spelling for Tel Abib. Abib was the old Hebrew first month of the year, the month of the Passover. It was also the month of Israel's new beginning as they left Egypt. The months were renamed and the calendar changed during the Babylonian captivity. Just as Daniel and his three Hebrew companions were given Babylonian names, so too were the Jewish months.

Modern Tel Aviv as seen from Jaffa

Along with the return of Jews were some misguided Christian groups, even evangelicals, who were going to help Israel bring in the messianic Kingdom. However, the Jews purchased land to develop the *kibbutz* system. The *kibbutzim* were actually Jewish enclaves where the returnees could not only develop an independent agricultural community, but maintain and expand their cultural influence. The *kibbutz* was actually a communist cell on an enormous scale. This was the way the Jews bought back the land, and gradually refounded a Jewish entity that began to resemble the Old Testament example.

Great Britain gained control and became the protectorate of Palestine after World War One. The Arabs became alarmed over the continual purchase of land by Jews, and as reported in the January 30, 1936, edition of the *Palestine Post,* the Arab party political leaders petitioned England to:

1. Establish a democratic government in Palestine;
2. Halt Jewish immigration completely; and
3. Make it illegal for any Arab or Palestinian to sell land, buildings, or property to any Jew.

The headline in the same edition of the *Palestine Post* read: **"Land Sales Restrictions Announced by Sir Arthur, High Commissioner."** The British commissioner, giving in to Arab demands, prohibited any further Jewish immigration and placed restrictions on further sales of land to Jews. This was a cruel act by England, as on the same page of the *Palestine Post* was news that Nazi persecution of the Jews had reached genocidal proportions. Their escape route to their Jewish homeland had been cut off by Great Britain.

Nevertheless, by this time the population of Tel Aviv had increased to one hundred twenty-five thousand, and the *kibbutz* system was solidly established. The Jews had returned and bought up the land and sealed their deeds. The land was rightfully theirs, and a solid base had been established for a future return of more Jews and the establishing of a Jewish nation. Another prophetic sign of the coming Messianic Age was being fulfilled.

Restored Cities' Biblical Identification

The thirty-sixth and thirty-seventh chapters of Ezekiel appear to refer to the period of the return up to the Tribulation, or the "time of Jacob's trouble." We read about some of the specifics of the return and the resettlement of the Promised Land in Ezekiel 36:11, 24:

> And I will multiply upon you man and beast; and they shall increase and bring fruit: and I will settle you after your old estates, and will do better unto you than at your beginnings . . . For I will take you from among the heathen, and gather you out of all countries, and will bring you into your own land.

We read also this latter-day promise in Isaiah 44:26: ". . . Thou shalt be inhabited; and to the cities of Judah, Ye shall be built, and I will raise up the decayed places thereof."

We associate the cities of Israel with their biblical names. However, we have to remember that after A.D. 70 the Romans were in control of the cities, and many were given Roman names; then the Muslims came in and renamed some of the cities with Muslim or Arab names; then the Crusaders were in the land for two hundred years; then the Byzantines and the Turks. During the Byzantine period, cities in the land would be given names like Reshat, Fahma, Seilum, Amud, etc. But the promise to Israel was that when the Lord gathered them back into the land, the cities would be named and settled according to their old biblical names and in the same location.

Modern Be'ersheva

In going through Israel today, the tourist will find that Nazareth is Nazareth, Cana is Cana, Be'ersheva is Be'ersheva, Elath is Elath, and even the little village of Nain is called Nain today. Almost without exception the cities have been renamed with their biblical names and settled in the same places as they were in Bible times. This is indeed another remarkable messianic sign today in Israel.

WHY THREE CITIES WERE NOT RESETTLED

In discussing the messianic promise that the cities of Israel would be settled and renamed after their old estates, we concluded that this had been done as the Jews began to return to their land at the turn of the twentieth century. However, Jesus said that there would be three cities in Israel that would never be inhabited again. This prophecy is found in Matthew 11:20–21, 23:

> Then began he to upbraid the cities wherein most of his mighty works were done, because they repented not: Woe unto thee, Chorazin! woe unto thee, Bethsaida! for if the mighty works, which were done in you, had been done in Tyre and Sidon, they would have repented long ago in sackcloth and ashes. . . . And thou, Capernaum, which art exalted unto heaven, shalt be brought down to hell: for if the mighty works, which have been done in thee, had been done in Sodom, it would have remained until this day.

We read in Matthew 9:1 that Capernaum was Jesus' "own city." After Jesus was rejected at Nazareth and the men of that city tried to kill Him, He went to Capernaum. Jesus indicated that Capernaum was a large and prosperous city—that it was exalted to Heaven. The city was on the main road from Jerusalem that went along the northern shore of the Sea of Galilee and continued to Damascus. The Romans had a tariff station at Capernaum and Matthew was a tax collector. But it was here that Jesus had relatives, and it was here that He called His apostles.

Jesus did not have a home in Capernaum, or even a house to live in. He said that He did not even have His own place to lay His head. The Scriptures indicate that most of the time He must have lived with Peter's family. Although Peter was hot tempered and impetuous, he must have been a good husband, because he suffered his mother–in–law to live with him. Paul also indicated that when Peter went abroad he took his wife with him. It was in this area that Jesus gave the Sermon on the Mount, calmed the waves of the sea, divided the loaves and fishes to feed thousands, and so many came to Him to be healed at Peter's house that the sick and lame were let down through the roof. The foundation of Peter's house is still in evidence today.

The good news, according to John the Baptist, was "repent, for the kingdom of heaven is at hand." This was also the Gospel of the Kingdom that Jesus declared. But even though the people of Capernaum

Ruins of Capernaum

witnessed Jesus' miracles, heard His message, and saw the hundreds that He healed, they did not repent. They did not accept Him as the Messiah. Jesus said that if He had done the same miracles in Sodom, even that wicked and evil city would have repented, and so He pronounced a curse upon the city. Capernaum is one of the biblical cities in Israel that has not been rebuilt or resettled. It is still in ruins.

Another city that Jesus cursed was Bethsaida. From the biblical description, it appears that Bethsaida was located at the northeast corner of the Sea of Galilee where the Jordan empties into the sea, and near the land of the Gadarenes, which is on the east side. Peter evidently lived in Bethsaida before he moved to Capernaum. Bethsaida was also the home of Philip and Andrew, and it was here that Jesus walked on the water to the boat carrying the disciples. This miracle is recorded in Mark 6:48. Jesus did other miracles and presented messianic signs to the inhabitants of Bethsaida, but like those at Capernaum, they neither repented nor received Him as the promised Messiah. There are only a few blocks of masonry sticking out of the ground that marks the site of Bethsaida. It has, as Jesus prophesied, not been rebuilt.

Another city that Jesus cursed was Chorazin. Chorazin was located approximately five miles north of Capernaum on top of a mountain. The Bible mentions no one of importance as coming from this city, nor is there any record of Jesus even visiting Chorazin. We know that it was a fairly large town for that time. It had a large and well built synagogue, as well as many other buildings. However, Jesus or some of the apostles and disciples must have given a powerful witness in that city to deserve such a curse upon it. Today, Chorazin is a scene of utter desolation.

Chorazin is somewhat of a mystery, because it was evidently a beautiful city, and it is amazing that it was built in a volcanic area where there was no agriculture and no water. Only Jesus mentioned Chorazin, and it was not even referred to by Josephus. We must assume its importance to the ministry of Jesus is referred to in John 21:25.

It is amazing indeed that everything concerning the return of the Jews and the resettling of the land is exactly as prophesied in every detail. If all these prophecies have been fulfilled to date, then we know the few yet–to–be fulfilled prophecies will also come to pass, including the Great Tribulation, the Battle of Armageddon, and the literal return of Jesus Christ from Heaven. We live in exciting days in this last generation before Jesus comes.

SIGN NUMBER 27

THE PROPHETIC REBIRTH OF ISRAEL

One of the most impressive messianic signs is the refounding of Israel as a nation on May 14, 1948.

We note again that the main concern of the prophets of Israel was the arrival of the Messianic age in which all the covenants God made with the fathers would be honored and every promise to the nation fulfilled. The prophet Isaiah arrived at the grand finale in the last chapter of his book of prophecy: "For, behold, the LORD will come with fire, and with his chariots like a whirlwind, to render his anger with fury, and his rebuke with flames of fire" (Isaiah 66:15).

Basic Jewish and Christian eschatology agree in the manner the Messiah will appear and what will follow in the wake of His coming. The difference is that the vast majority of the Jews from the time of Jesus to the present have never accepted Him as the promised Messiah. Observing Jews look for the coming Messiah; Christians look for Jesus Christ the Messiah to come again. In any event, from a Jewish perspective the nation must be refounded before the Messiah would come; from a Christian position the nation of Israel must be refounded before Jesus Christ will bodily return to this earth. Jesus Christ in the Olivet Discourse describes His return in much the same manner as Isaiah describes the Messiah's coming, which also coincides with the coming of the King of Kings as foretold by the apostle John in Revelation 19.

A day of Shabbat at the Western Wall

Before the coming of the Lord to put down all enemies and establish His Kingdom, Isaiah referred to a preceding event that would happen:

> Before she travailed, she brought forth; before her pain came, she was delivered of a man child. Who hath heard such a thing? who hath seen such things? Shall the earth be made to bring forth in one day? or shall a nation be born at once? for as soon as Zion travailed, she brought forth her children. Shall I bring to the birth, and not cause to bring forth? saith the LORD: shall I cause to bring forth, and shut the womb? saith thy God.
>
> —Isaiah 66:7–9

Christian theologians present the explanation that the man–child which Israel brought forth before there were any birthpangs was Jesus Christ. There was no travail in birth because Israel never recognized Him. However, the prophet continued to describe Israel's travail in the birth of the nation that would be born in a day. This event, according to the context of the prophecy, would occur before the Lord's coming. We believe this prophecy had a fulfillment on May 14, 1948.

The headline of the *Palestine Post* of May 16, 1948, read: **"State of Israel Is Born."** The newspaper account read in part:

> The first independent Jewish state in nineteen centuries was born in Tel Aviv as the British Mandate over Palestine came to an end at midnight on Friday, and it was immediately subjected to the test of fire. As the State of Israel was proclaimed, the battle for Jerusalem raged, with most of the city falling to the Jews. At the same time, President Truman announced that the United States would accord recognition of the new State. A few hours later, Palestine was invaded by Moslem armies from the south, east, and north.

General George Marshall, spokesman for the U.S. State Department, had wired the premier of the new State of Israel, David Ben Gurion, that if he declared an independent state, that five Arab armies would immediately march against the new nation and within three days there would not be a Jew left alive in Palestine. However, the prophet Isaiah twenty-seven hundred years before had prophesied that God would not allow this to happen. He wrote: "Shall I bring to the birth, and not cause to bring forth? saith the LORD: shall I cause to bring forth, and shut the womb? saith thy God." The prophet also promised, ". . . as soon as Zion travailed, she brought forth her children." General Marshall was wrong because he had not read Isaiah 66. A ragtag Jewish army with few arms and little training defeated five well-trained and fully equipped armies with artillery, planes, and tanks from five Arab nations. As prophesied, Jews from all nations afterward began to return. Nothing like this had ever happened before. After being scattered into all nations for over nineteen centuries, a remnant returns and immediately becomes a nation.

The Prophetic Order of the Jews' Return Fulfilled

It is beyond reason how any person of average intelligence could connect the dots of what God has prophesied for Israel in the last days and to what has actually occurred and not understand, or at least reach a reasonable conclusion, that we must be living in the last days of the last days, and Jesus is coming soon.

Egypt in the Bible is given as an example of the world, or a type of world, and God demonstrated His will and His power in bringing the children of Israel to the Promised Land. God is once more demonstrating His will and His power in bringing them out of the world back into the land He gave them. In addition, not only is God bringing them back as prophesied, even more miraculous, the prophet Isaiah foretold the exact order of their return.

> For I am the LORD thy God, the Holy One of Israel, thy Saviour: I gave Egypt for thy ransom, Ethiopia and Seba for thee. Since thou wast precious in my sight, thou hast been honourable, and I have loved thee: therefore will I give men for thee, and people for thy life. Fear not: for I am with thee: I will bring thy seed from the [1] east, and gather thee from the [2] west; I will say to the [3] north, Give up; and to the [4] south, Keep not back: bring my sons from far, and my daughters from the ends of the earth; . . . Ye are my witnesses, saith the LORD, and my servant whom I have chosen: that ye may know and believe me, and understand that I am he: before me there was no God formed, neither shall there be after me. . . . This people have I formed for myself; they shall shew forth my praise. But thou hast not called upon me, O Jacob; but thou hast been weary of me, O Israel.
>
> —Isaiah 43:3–6, 10, 21–22

European Jews, Chinese Jews, and Ethiopian Jews returning to Israel from the 1950s to 1980s.

Isaiah prophesied that though Israel would not believe, when the time for the Messiah was at hand, the Lord would regather them in their unbelief. Israel would first return from the east, and according to the *Judaic Encyclopedia,* in 1900 there were three hundred thousand Jews in Turkey; in 1939, there were only thirty thousand. The same percentages of Jewish immigration to Israel also applied to Jordan, Syria, Iraq, Yemen, and other nations in the Middle East.

The second stage of Jewish immigration came from the west, the nations of Europe. In 1939 the Jewish population of Europe was 9,408,000; in 1948, it had dropped to 3,708,000. After the Nazi Holocaust in which almost 6 million Jews were killed, additional thousands fled to Israel seeking a place of peace and safety.

Liberated Jews after Holocaust as they are dispersed to various countries.

The third phase of Jewish immigration, according to prophecy, was to come from the north. Until the *glasnost* policies of Gorbachev were initiated in Russia in 1988, the Jews were not allowed to emigrate. Then, a few began to return through Helsinki; but the prime minister of Finland closed the exit door because of Arab pressure. A constituent of our ministry, Siiki, and a friend of the prime minister's wife, informed him that unless he opened the door to Jewish emigration from Russia again, God would do to him what He did to the king of Edom. To date, over four hundred thousand Russian Jews have gone to Israel.

The fourth and final phase of the return of a remnant to prepare for the coming of Messiah would be from the south, according to Isaiah. In 1991 approximately fourteen thousand black Jews (Falasha) were flown out of Ethiopia to Israel in Operation Solomon. According to tradition, the black Jews of Ethiopia are descendants of a son born to the Queen of Sheba by Solomon (1 Kings 10). Thus, the order of the return of a Jewish remnant to await Messiah's appearance is exactly as prophesied.

Matthew 8:11 clearly is a reference to Gentile participation in the Kingdom of Heaven, the Messianic Age. In this scripture Jesus mentioned only two directions, the east and the west. Luke 13:29 indicates a separation or a difference between saved Jews and unsaved Jews. Here it would seem that Jesus is referring to a regathering of those Jews acceptable for the Kingdom Age, and in this scripture all four directions are mentioned in the same order given by Isaiah: east, west, north, and south.

In taking Bible tours to Israel, I am always fascinated by finding out from individual Jews what nation they came from and why they returned. I believe it has now been confirmed that Jews have returned from every nation in the world. The latest population figures indicate a current population of 7.25 million—6 million Jews and approximately 1.25 million Arabs. When I was in Baghdad in 1978, Saddam Hussein had just hanged eight Jews in the streets with signs on their bodies, "JEWS GO HOME." Even though most Jews have returned from many countries because of persecution, in due course it will be revealed to them the real reason, which is to say "Blessed is He who comes in the name of the Lord" when Jesus returns.

Restoring the Shekel

The Jews came back to Israel with all kinds of currency—francs, dollars, pounds, rubles, etc. Merchants were having a difficult time buying and selling because there was no basic exchange unit. Finally, they returned to their traditional and biblical money that Abraham, Isaac, and Jacob would have had on their persons.

The first Hebrew unit of monetary exchange, the shekel, is first mentioned in Genesis 23:15. Abraham bought a burial site for Sarah at a cost of four hundred shekels. A shekel is approximately one-third of an ounce of silver. Today, the land would be worth approximately eighteen hundred dollars. A talent is three thousand shekels of silver. It is thought that the first silver or gold coins to appear were in Assyria at about 900 B.C. It is possible that a shekel could have been either a minted coin predating the Assyrian coins, or it could have been a silver nugget of about one-third of an ounce.

We read in Exodus 30:11–16, that every Israelite male of the age of twenty years or older had to make an offering of one-half shekel to maintain services in the tabernacle. However, according to Ezekiel 45:12, the offering to the temple required by each Israelite could run as high as sixty shekels of silver. When Israel became a nation in 1948, there was no national currency. The British pound or the U.S. dollar were the most common monies used for exchange units. Finally in 1980 the Knesset restored the shekel as the official unit of exchange in Israel. We read from Ezekiel 45:12–13, 16: "And the shekel shall be twenty gerahs. . . . This is the oblation that ye shall offer. . . . All the people of the land shall give this oblation for the prince in Israel."

The restoration of the shekel was an important messianic sign because, according to Ezekiel, when the Messiah appears offerings and oblations must be made in shekels.

Although the restoring of the shekel as the basic monetary unit in Israel may seem to be a relatively unimportant event, it shows that every jot and tittle of the prophetic Word must be fulfilled so that no one on Judgment Day can complain they didn't know because God left something out in His prophetic signs concerning the last generation.

Reviving the Ancient Hebrew Language

Another problem with the reviving of a country after almost two thousand years was communication. As it was at Babel, someone would ask for a bagel and they would be given a brick.

After A.D. 70 when the majority of Jews in Israel were scattered into all nations during the Diaspora, they learned or adopted the language of the country in which they lived. While many Jews over the centuries continued to speak their national language, the Hebrew gradually became even more corrupted. At the turn of the twentieth century as more and more Jews began to migrate back to Israel there was a problem in that they could not communicate. They either spoke different languages, or a Hebrew dialect that was not readily or commonly understood. In 1928 a Jew by the name of Eliezer Ben Yehuda, evidently with the backing of the Zionist Organization, got Hebrew recognized as the official language of the return. This was also foretold as a messianic sign in Zephaniah 3:8–10:

> Therefore wait ye upon me, saith the Lord, until the day that I rise up to the prey: for my determination is to gather the nations, that I may assemble the kingdoms, to pour upon them mine indignation, even all my fierce anger: for all the earth shall be devoured with the fire of my jealousy. For then will I turn to the people a pure language, that they may all call upon the name of the Lord, to serve him with one consent. From beyond the rivers of Ethiopia my suppliants, even the daughter of my dispersed, shall bring mine offering.

This prophecy definitely has a latter–day setting when the Jews began returning from all nations. The time is given prior to the Battle of Armageddon. The prophet indicated that even the Jews who return from Ethiopia, or beyond Ethiopia, will have to learn Hebrew. The black Jews from Ethiopia today in Israel speak Hebrew like everyone else.

In the midst of a billion hostile Muslim neighbors, this tiny nation outnumbered 100 to 1 has to be one of consent in order to survive. Even here in the United States in making a telephone call, the operator will ask what language you speak. The one important item on which Jews are not in one consent is, of course, the identity of their Messiah, but we know that Jesus will take care of that when He returns.

Sign Number 28

The Trees of Israel

The Fig Tree

If we were to list all the signs in the Bible identifiable with the last days, latter years, or Kingdom of Heaven in order of importance, we would have to place the return of the remnant of Israel and refounding of the nation as number one.

A primary sign of the end of the age is the budding of the fig tree, the rebirth of the nation of Israel as the budding of a tender branch.

In numerous scriptures trees are used as symbols or examples of nations. In the ninth chapter of Judges we read where the trees in due time determined to anoint a king, or one specific tree, over them. The first tree that was approached with the offer of the Kingdom was the "olive tree," symbolic of spiritual Israel under the judges: "The LORD called thy name, A green olive tree . . ." (Jeremiah 11:16).

According to Judges 9:9, the olive tree was unwilling or unable to fulfill its calling and appointment. Next, we read that the trees counseled and called for the fig tree to accept the position and bring in the Kingdom, but the fig tree also was unwilling or unable to accept. After the era of the judges, Israel said, "Anoint us a king," so the fig tree represented national Israel under the era of the kings. Israel is referred to in many scriptures as God's fig tree (Joel 1:7; Jeremiah 8:13; etc.). However, we read in Judges 9:11 that the fig tree was either unable or unwilling to serve as ruler over the nations, representative of the Kingdom Age.

Next, the trees ask the lowly grape vine to be the ruler over the nations, but even the vine was so self–centered it would not serve in a Kingdom position. The vine is symbolic of messianic Israel, the four hundred years after the prophet Malachi when a forerunner of the Messiah would appear to prepare his way (Malachi 3:1). The prophet Zechariah also referenced the coming Messiah as "The BRANCH" (Zechariah 6:12). Jesus fully understood that He was offering Himself to Israel as the Messiah when He stated in John 15:1, "I am the true vine. . . ." But the citizens of Israel said of Jesus, "We will not have this man to reign over us" (Luke 19:14).

According to the Abrahamic covenant, Israel is to be head of all nations, so finally the nations looked to Israel and concluded the only candidate left to consider was the abominable bramble bush:

> Then said all the trees unto the bramble, Come thou, and reign over us. And the bramble said unto the trees, If in truth ye anoint me king over you, then come and put your trust in my shadow: and if not, let fire come out of the bramble, and devour the cedars of Lebanon.
>
> —Judges 9:14–15

In the parable of the trees it is evident that the "bramble bush" represents the false messiah, also referred to as the coming Antichrist, or anti–Messiah. The prophet Daniel referred to the "abomination of desolation" repeatedly; Jesus, Paul, and John in the New Testament referenced the prophecy by Daniel. The false messiah presents himself as the true Messiah, and when the world does not universally worship him as God, the fires of desolation follow. The cedars of Lebanon will be burned up (Jeremiah 22:7), Egypt will be desolate for forty years and, according to Revelation, all grass and one–third of the trees will be burned up.

During the Diaspora, the olive tree has been cut down, but the roots of an olive tree never die. According to Romans 11, when the Church Age expires, Israel will be grafted back into the roots. In Israel today the dormant vine of messianic expectations is again putting forth new branches, and the fig tree, representative of national Israel, has budded again.

In looking forward to coming judgments against his nation, Jeremiah prophesied:

> . . . therefore shall they fall among them that fall: **in the time of their visitation** they shall be cast down, saith the LORD. I will surely consume them, saith the LORD: there shall be no grapes on the vine, nor figs on the fig tree, and the leaf shall fade; and the things that I have given them shall pass away from them.
>
> —Jeremiah 8:12–13

Jesus proposed that the time of this desolation would begin with Him:

> For the days shall come upon thee, that thine enemies shall cast a trench about thee, and compass thee round, and keep thee in on every side, And shall lay thee even with the ground, and thy children within thee; and they shall not leave in thee one stone upon another; because **thou knewest not the time of thy visitation.**
>
> —Luke 19:43–44

Fig trees grow in abundance in Israel

There are two seasons of figs in Israel. As brought out by the *Fausset Bible Dictionary and Encyclopedia,* the winter figs ripen at about the time of the Passover. The leaves on the fig trees are just beginning to appear as the figs become sweet enough to eat. The fall figs ripen at about the time of Yom Kippur, and the second crop is the sweeter and more abundant harvest.

When Jesus came to Jerusalem, He stayed at the home of Mary, Martha, and Lazarus in Bethany. He would go over the Mount of Olives, through the Kidron Valley, and enter the city through one of the gates on the east wall.

The Mount of Olives is not only known for the olive trees that have historically grown on it, but also for the fig trees. Between Bethany and Jerusalem on the Mount of Olives lies a small village called Beit Pagi, which is known to Christians as Beth Page. *Pagi* in Hebrew are the young, unripe figs. This is definitely an indication for fig trees that grew and still grow on the mountain.

During the week before His crucifixion, Jesus daily traveled from Bethany to Jerusalem, and we read of one event that involved figs in Matthew 21:18–20:

> Now in the morning as he returned into the city, he hungered. And when he saw a fig tree in the way, he came to it, and found nothing thereon, but leaves only, and said unto it, Let no fruit grow on thee henceforward for ever. And presently the fig tree withered away. And when the disciples saw it, they marvelled, saying, How soon is the fig tree withered away!

It was not time for the fig tree to be fully leafed, but even so, it should have been heavy with sweet fruit. In this object lesson, Jesus was evidently teaching the disciples by example that Israel was lacking in spiritual maturity for the Kingdom Age. Fig leaves, as in the example of Adam and Eve, are representative of self–righteousness (Isaiah 64:6). The fulfillment of this prophecy in type occurred in A.D. 70.

However, this one example in no way supports covenant theology or replacement theology, to wit that the church has forever replaced Israel as God's earthly people. Jesus later taught within the context of the Olivet Discourse:

> Now learn a parable of the fig tree; When his branch is yet tender, and putteth forth leaves, ye know that summer is nigh: So likewise ye, when ye shall see all these things, know that it is near, even at the doors.
>
> —Matthew 24:32–33

The primary concern of the disciples was the restoration of the kingdom of Israel and the fulfillment of the messianic promises (Acts 1:6). Messianic concerns were also addressed by Jesus to John the Baptist. In the Olivet Discourse Jesus referred to the prophecies given Daniel, and then added others as signs in the Church Age, the primary one being the budding of the fig tree, the rebirth of the nation of Israel as the budding of a tender branch. The fig trees in Israel are budding, putting on fruit again, and some growing to thirty or even forty feet high. The sign of the fig tree is also coming to pass in that Israel has once more become a nation, holding forth a promise of the soon arrival of the Kingdom Age.

Not only is Israel the apple of God's eye, the fig tree, an emblem of Israel, is His favorite one in the forest. And the next time that Jesus walks from the Mount of Olives to the Golden Gate and passes a fig tree, I am sure He will find figs on it. Nevertheless, the abundant and luxuriant fig trees growing again in Israel today are a sign that tiny Israel will soon fulfill its destined covenant role in being a blessing to all nations as God ordained when He said to Abraham, "I will bless them that bless thee."

The Trees of Prophecy

Moses warned the Israelites before they crossed over the Jordan that water would be scarce and there would be only one rainy season. In 1400 B.C. at the time of the exodus, there were forests in Israel, especially in the north. The forests and groves of Israel are mentioned many times in Isaiah, Jeremiah, and Ezekiel. But the best lumber for building purposes came from Lebanon. However, Solomon planted trees throughout much of Israel.

We read about Solomon's environmental project in Ecclesiastes 2:4–6:

> I made me great works; I builded me houses; I planted me vine-

yards: I made me gardens and orchards, and I planted trees in them of all kind of fruits: I made me pools of water, to water therewith the wood that bringeth forth trees.

Beautiful ancient olive tree in front of the dining commons at the Weizmann Institute.

The tribe of Dan was given the land between the section allotted to the tribe of Judah and the Mediterranean. However, this land had few trees and very little water. In addition, the Danites had to continually fight the Philistines. So finally, the entire tribe moved to the area in the north along the Dan River. They developed the city of Dan where there were many trees, some parts a veritable jungle. The fact that the tribe of Dan did not have faith to claim the land God gave them may be one reason why the Scriptures indicate Dan's part in the messianic Kingdom may be small. In any event, we know that for large trees to grow in Israel in areas south of the Sea of Galilee they had to be watered during the dry season.

The destruction of Israel's forests began in A.D. 70 with Titus. According to Josephus, so many Jews were crucified during the siege of Jerusalem that there was not enough room for crosses, nor wood enough to crucify those Titus condemned to death (*Fausset's Dictionary,* 145). Even the olive trees on Mount Olivet were used for crosses. According to Josephus, the Romans lay siege to Jerusalem at the time of the Passover when the number in the city would have been three times the regular population. Josephus estimated that there were 2.5 million Jews in the city at the time, not counting foreigners, lepers, or women in their monthly cycle (*Wars of the Jews,* book VI, chapter 9). 1.1 million died in the siege, mostly by starvation. After the city fell, the priests and Levites pleaded for their lives, but Titus concluded that as the temple had been destroyed, there was no need for them, so he ordered their throats to be cut. Next, Titus ordered all the elderly and sick to be killed. According to Josephus, the Roman soldiers killed so many with their swords they could no longer lift their arms. Titus saved some of the best looking and tallest Jews to be bound as captives and be a part of the parade when he made his triumphant entry into Rome. Titus sent ninety-seven thousand who were still able to work into the mines in Egypt. The rest he sent to be sold on the slave markets in Alexandria, or to the many theatres throughout the Roman Empire to die as gladiators or to fight with wild beasts for the entertainment of Roman citizens (*Wars of the Jews,* book VI, chapter 9).

The Romans were unmerciful to those who opposed them, and this is why the defenders of Gamla and Masada committed suicide rather than surrender. While Josephus attempted to present Titus as a just and honorable man, it is difficult to justify his acts of extreme cruelty, especially the daily crucifixion of thousands of Jews during the siege. The reason for presenting these specific incidents in the account of the fall of Jerusalem is that the trees of Israel symbolically represented their long sufferings from A.D. 70 until the return. The Romans cut down the trees of Israel for crosses and war machines, like battering rams and catapults. The Muslims cut down the trees to build their mosques; the Crusaders cut down the trees for firewood and to use in the construction of their castles. The Turks cut down the trees to use as ties for their railroads and firewood to stoke their engines. When the Jews began to return at the turn of the century there were no trees on the mountains and only a few in cities like Jericho. But we read this messianic promise:

> But thou, Israel, art my servant, Jacob whom I have chosen, the seed of Abraham my friend. Thou whom I have taken from the ends of the earth, and called thee from the chief men thereof, and said unto thee, Thou art my servant; I have chosen thee, and not cast thee away. Fear thou not; for I am with thee: be not dismayed; for I am thy God: I will strengthen thee; yea, I will help thee; yea, I will uphold thee with the right hand of my righteousness. . . . I will plant in the wilderness the cedar, the shittah tree, and the myrtle, and the oil tree; I will set in the desert the fir tree, and the pine, and the box tree together: That they may see, and know, and consider, and understand together, that the hand of the LORD hath done this, and the Holy One of Israel hath created it.
>
> —Isaiah 41:8–10, 19–20

Acacia tree in the Negev desert in Israel

Isaiah prophesied that God would never ultimately forsake Israel. A sign to Israel at the return would be the reforestation of the bare hills and valleys of the land. When the nations would see the myrtle tree, the oil tree, the fir trees, the pine trees, when the nations of the world would see trees growing in the mountains of Israel in such numbers and kinds that have never grown there before, they were to know, consider, and understand, that this is the Lord's doing. It is a sign to the nations that the times of the Gentiles are coming to an end, and God is once more preparing Israel for its role in the coming messianic Kingdom. Our ministry has planted two forests in Israel, one in the Valley of Elah where

David slew Goliath. On every mission tour to Israel we try to give the members an opportunity to plant a tree in Israel.

I tell my tour members when they plant a tree in Israel they are helping to fulfill prophecy. In fact, I also tell them when they spend their money in Israel they are also helping to fulfill prophecy because Isaiah said the wealth of the Gentiles will pour unto thee. Everywhere we look to Israel today, whether in the daily news or walking through the land, we are immersed in the promise of God that Jesus is coming soon.

SIGN NUMBER 29

THE VULTURES OF ISRAEL

For centuries there were no vultures in Israel and very few other kinds of birds. The reason for this was simple; the forests had been destroyed and there was very little grass and other types of foliage. God made the vultures for a reason. That reason was to eat animals that had died and therefore keep the land clean of garbage and disease. However, when there are no animals to die, there are no vultures. Today in Israel, on the east side of the land of Gadarenes and the lower levels of the Golan Heights at Gamla, there are hundreds of vultures.

It is symbolic that Gamla is where the vultures nest and raise their young. Gamla was built in the fork of a deep canyon, which is one thousand feet deep. From the side of the canyon there is a land protrusion called the "Camel Hump." Some of those who returned from Babylon built a small city on the Camel Hump because below was water, and the site was easily defended.

When Josephus began the rebellion against the Romans in A.D. 66 in Galilee, his defense line was anchored on the west by Mount Tabor and on the east by Gamla. When the Roman army commanded by General Vespasian moved against Gamla, the people of the area fled to the city, increasing the population greatly. Josephus himself in *The Wars of the Jews,* book four, chapter one, gave a description of Gamla and how he built up the defenses. He also gave a detailed description of the battle. Vespasian's first attempt to take the city ended in disaster, and he lost a large number of his soldiers. He called up reinforcements and finally took Gamla, killing four thousand Jews in the battle. The women and children, seeing that the battle was lost, threw themselves into the canyon below. The number who committed suicide at Gamla was said by Josephus to have been five thousand.

Vulture at Gamla

Vespasian's son, Captain Titus, was in command of the assault on Mount Tabor. Again, according to Josephus, the women and children taken at Mount Tabor stretched out for two miles along the road, the number totaling nine thousand. Titus commanded his soldiers to begin killing them, and six thousand women and children were killed by the sword. He evidently spared three thousand as an act of mercy. But this is why the Jews would commit suicide rather than surrender to the Romans. It is symbolic as well as prophetic that the vultures have returned to Gamla. Isaiah placed the return of the vultures to Israel in a messianic setting:

> Come near, ye nations, to hear; and hearken, ye people: let the earth hear, and all that is therein; the world, and all things that come forth of it. For the indignation of the LORD is upon all nations, and his fury upon all their armies: he hath utterly destroyed them, he hath delivered them to the slaughter. Their slain also shall be cast out, and their stink shall come up out of their carcases, and the mountains shall be melted with their blood. . . . For it is the day of the LORD's vengeance, and the year of recompences for the controversy of Zion. . . . There shall the great owl make her nest, and lay, and hatch, and gather under her shadow: there shall the vultures also be gathered, every one with her mate.
>
> —Isaiah 34:1–3, 8, 15

During the spring and fall migration seasons, billions of birds fly through Israel, because Israel is a natural land bridge between Africa and Europe and Asia. This is one reason why we might conclude that the Battle of Armageddon will be in the spring or fall. We read about the armies of the nations who will be killed at Armageddon in Revelation 19: "And I saw an angel standing in the sun; and he cried with a loud voice, saying to all the fowls that fly in the midst of heaven, Come and gather yourselves together unto the supper of the great God . . . and all the fowls were filled with their flesh" (Revelation 19:17, 21).

Many kinds of predatory birds like eagles, crows, gulls, blue jays, and others eat meat. Doubtless, the vultures will also be involved in the aftermath of Armageddon.

The Scriptures indicate to us that the battle of Ezekiel chapters thirty–eight and thirty–nine will also be during the Tribulation period, or the time of Jacob's trouble. Ezekiel 39:17 indicates that many during this invasion from the north will fall upon the Golan Heights, the biblical land of Bashan:

> . . . thus saith the Lord God; Speak unto every feathered fowl, and to every beast of the field, Assemble yourselves, and come; gather yourselves on every side to my sacrifice that I do sacrifice for you, even a great sacrifice upon the mountains of Israel, that ye may eat flesh, and drink blood. Ye shall eat the flesh of the mighty, and drink the blood of the princes of the earth, of rams, of lambs, and of goats, of bullocks, all of them fatlings of Bashan.
>
> —Ezekiel 39:17–18

It is amazing that the vulture population is exploding in the foothills of the mountains of Bashan, now known as the Golan Heights. The Israeli air force will not allow planes or helicopters to fly over Gamla during the vulture's nesting seasons.

It is interesting that Israel has almost adopted the vulture as its national bird. Perhaps this is because at the Battle of Armageddon the vulture will be the winged messenger of revenge for all that the Jews have suffered. It is also interesting that prior to the Battle of Armageddon that vultures will be nesting in Israel, every one with their mate. The overseer of the Gamla Park told me personally that the vultures were not only laying twice as many eggs as they usually do, but they are laying four times as many. I am going to defer to Gilla Treibich for verification.

■ ■ ■ ■ ■

I do not believe the Gamla Park Authority was exaggerating. The Gamla River with its canyons is the home of the largest number of birds of prey. The river provides a perfect habitat for nesting because of the many hiding places and availability of food. Every year forty or fifty couples of various birds of prey nest here; of that number twenty to thirty are griffon vultures. In addition, there are short–toed eagles, Egyptian vultures,

Bonelli's eagles, kestrel falcons, and at night one can spot eagle owls.

The most impressive beyond any doubt is the griffon vulture. Its wingspan reaches nine feet and enables the bird to hover in place for a long time while looking for food. This vulture can weigh up to twenty-two pounds. Its color is brown, and when it is mature there are speckles of black on the wings. At the age of five or six the vulture reaches maturity and can start to reproduce. These birds stay in flocks, and they are faithful to their friends as well as to their homes. They can accumulate up to five pounds of meat in their stomach, and thus do not need to eat again for a day or two. The nesting period is in the fall, and then one can see in the air beautiful courting dances of the couples. Both partners build the nest and both share in the setting of the eggs until they hatch. The parents are very devoted. They feed the young ones and protect them with their bodies from cold and heat. The young vulture will stay in the nest almost four months before it flies away and becomes independent (Gamla Nature and Landscape, *Ofer and Liora Bahat, 1991, 64–66).*

A visit to Gamla is always a highlight. In the afternoon there are usually a great number of birds that come out and fly over the antiquities and over the canyon. This, and the many other animals that have returned to Israel, is another sign that Israel is being restored. The birds and wild animals were absent from the land for many, many centuries, but now that they are back, the land again is becoming what God wanted it to be. As far as the vultures are concerned, they are an unbelievable phenomenon.

There was a project inaugurated in Israel several years ago sponsored by our electric company. Some vultures were fitted with positional microphones. The microphones allow scientists to follow the movements of the vultures. One of them reached as far as Istanbul, Turkey, in two days. This is a distance of several hundred miles. Some of the vultures were running away, abandoning their nests, and some were found dead. The Golan Heights is a major area of military activity. On occasion, the vultures would swallow pieces of ammunition, or they would eat meat that had been killed with bullets. So the electric company, along with the Nature Preservation Society, made feeding stations for them and gave them good quality food. Now they are doing well in Gamla. The vulture population is exploding, and they are a joy to see.

You know, Israel is a very small country—only two hundred fifty miles long and just over sixty miles wide. This is a major problem for the air force, and the pilots always joke that they can't push the gas pedal to the ground because they'll be right outside of Israeli territory. Lots of training has to happen over the Golan Heights, and the helicopters in particular need to train in the ravines. The pilots also like to go into the canyons and "play." However, just as Dr. Hutchings said, there are explicit instructions from the air force commander that forbid flying over Gamla or any other nesting areas. The rangers of the Nature Society have an open direct line to the commander to report any violations.

—Gilla

. . . . .

KINGDOM AGE ANIMALS

In this chapter we will also consider the return of wild animal life to Israel. The prophetic Word indicates that wild animals, as mentioned in the Bible, would also return. During the Diaspora not only were there no vultures in Israel and very few birds, but wild animal life became practically extinct.

In the Old Testament, lions are mentioned over one hundred times, so we know there must have been lions in Israel. We read in Judges 14:8 that Samson killed a lion with his bare hands in Gaza, which would have been near the Mediterranean Sea and the Egyptian border. So if there were lions in Gaza, we know there must have been lions throughout the country. Jeremiah mentioned that it would be impossible for a leopard to change its spots, so we know there were leopards. Leopards are referred to in books other than Jeremiah. Wild goats (or ibex) and camels are mentioned; Job and Jeremiah mention ostriches; there were hares, or rabbits; coneys; wild ox, probably meaning wild water buffalo; fox; wolves; wild dogs (these were probably the dogs with round ears, not pointed ears); deer; bear; wild boar; weasels; and perhaps a few others mentioned in Scripture where the contemporary identification might be in doubt. Tile in a Byzantine church floor in Mount Nebo, dating to the fifth century, also shows giraffes and elephants, but it is difficult to find these animals identified by their names in the Old Testament.

Nubian ibex are plentiful in Israel.

With the Jews returning to Israel and the ecology of the land slowly being restored, wild animal life also began to return. We read in Ezekiel 39:17: ". . . Speak unto every feathered fowl, and to every beast of the field . . . that ye may eat flesh, and drink blood." The invasion from the north prophesied by Ezekiel is to occur after the Jews have returned to the land in "the latter years." This battle has to occur when there are wild beasts in Israel.

In the last two chapters of Isaiah the prophet looked forward to the final restoration of Israel, the coming of the Lord in fiery judgment, and

At Ein Gedi a sign is posted warning tourists what to do in the event they meet a leopard.

the messianic blessings upon all the people of Israel alive when the promised Kingdom arrives:

And I will rejoice in Jerusalem, and joy in my people: and the voice of weeping shall be no more heard in her, nor the voice of crying. . . . The wolf and the lamb shall feed together, and the lion shall eat straw like the bullock: and dust shall be the serpent's meat. They shall not hurt nor destroy in all my holy mountain, saith the LORD.

—Isaiah 65:19, 25

Some of the prophecies of the Bible relating to the Messianic Age could not be completed without the return of animal life as it was in Old Testament times.

At Gamla we have also seen fox, deer, ibex, coneys, and rabbits. One day I believe I saw a wolf. At Ein Gedi there are several types of animals in evidence, including deer, ibex, coneys, and there is a sign warning tourists what to do in the event that they meet a leopard. We have not heard of any lions or bears

Although we have not heard of any bears back in the land, with the restoration of the ecology, this too is possible.

At Ein Gedi, there are several types of animals in evidence. Dr. Hutchings believes he once saw a wolf there.

back in the land, but with the restoration of the ecology this too is possible.

It is amazing that the Lord has thought of every detail, even getting the birds and animals ready for the Second Coming of Jesus Christ. It is regrettable that in this last generation that no more of the world's inhabitants, including sleeping church members, are ready.

The white oryx is an impressive antelope with long horns. The oryx is one of the biggest animals in the antelope family. These beautiful creatures were almost hunted to extinction, but as a result of conservation efforts they have been saved and are now being returned to the wild.

The last time a lion was spotted in Israel was in 1960 by American archaeologist Nelson Gluck.

We have seen many fox at Gamla, as well as deer, ibex, coneys, and rabbits.

Sign Number 30

Water—

It Took a Miracle

The Sea of Galilee is one of the most beautiful natural lakes in the world. On my Bible tours to Israel, I insist upon a cruise on the lake where we anchor for fifteen minutes or so for a devotion. On one such devotional stop, I gave a brief dissertation on prayer and how God had miraculously answered prayer on former missions to China, Russia, and elsewhere we had served. Our guide was a brassy Jewish woman by the name of Audrey, who had made *alia* from Vancouver, Canada. When I finished my devotional, she remarked, "If you have such a direct pipeline to God, why don't you ask Him to give us cooler weather?"

It was in late September and still very hot for that time of the year. I replied, "Well, Audrey, we will include in our prayer the Lord's will concerning cooler weather. We know the Bible says the Jew requires a sign, so perhaps He will give us cooler weather if it be His will."

Audrey responded, "I don't want cooler weather next year or next month; I want cooler weather today."

"What time today?" I asked her.

"Twelve noon," she shot back.

"How much cooler do you want the temperature to be?" I asked again.

"Twenty degrees," she replied.

In our closing prayer after the devotional, I asked the Lord to consider Audrey's request and we thanked Him for His answer to our prayer, whatever was His will. We docked at the Jesus Boat Museum on the west side of the lake, and before we left the boat I asked Audrey, "If God gives us cooler weather at noon, will you accept Jesus Christ as Savior and be baptized in the Jordan River with the rest of the members who want to be baptized?"

Audrey replied, "It's a deal."

We exited the museum at exactly twelve noon; the wind changed to the north down the Arava, and the temperature dropped twenty degrees. Everyone looked at their watches. On the bus I reminded Audrey that baptisms would be that afternoon after the tour, and that we would stop by the hotel and she could get her bathing suit to be baptized. She angrily shouted, "Humph! You read the weather report!"

But that is the same kind of hard-hearted disbelief and rejection that Jesus encountered when He preached to the Jewish people the first time He came. He said that the Jews require a sign, but if even one would rise from the dead as a sign, they still would not believe. This same stubborn rejection is the mindset of 99 percent of the Jews today. This is why it will take the Great Tribulation to get them to cry out for Jesus Christ to come back.

Later I shared with a subsequent tour group the experience with Audrey, and they all looked at each other like I was telling a whopper. But Reuben Houston from New Orleans spoke up: "I was in that tour group, and Brother Hutchings is telling you the truth."

The Miracle of Increasing Rainfall

One of the objections raised before the League of Nations in considering endorsing the Balfour Declaration making so-called Palestine a home once more for the Jews was that there was not enough water to sustain a population of two or three million returning Jews. However, the population of Israel has now increased to 7.5 million, and there is still enough water. The Bible indicates that when the Jews come back in the last days, rainfall would increase correspondingly.

The book of Joel is about the coming Day of the Lord in which the nations will be judged during a time of tribulation, which would end with the annihilation of Israel's enemies.

Blow ye the trumpet in Zion, and sound an alarm in my holy mountain:

let all the inhabitants of the land tremble: for the day of the LORD cometh, for it is nigh at hand . . . Be glad then, ye children of Zion, and rejoice in the LORD your God: for he hath given you the former rain moderately, and he will cause to come down for you the rain, the former rain, and the latter rain in the first month.

—Joel 2:1, 23

In Bible times there were two seasons of rain in Israel: the fall and winter. During the Diaspora, as the Lord said, there was little rain. The average rainfall between 1931 and 1960 in the northern half of Israel was 21.1 inches a year. In 1980 the average rainfall in Israel was 29.1 inches, an increase of approximately 40 percent. The amazing phenomenon about the rainfall increase is that the percentage of increase has matched the percentage of increase in Jewish population during the past seventy years.

Ninety percent of the water needs of Israel come from the Sea of Galilee, a relatively small body of water approximately five miles wide and thirteen miles long. Without the Sea of Galilee, there would be no Israel. The water is very clean and pure, and even as the Jewish and Palestinian populations of Israel have increased from 1 million to 7 million, there is enough water for industry, household, and irrigational usage.

The prophet Hosea also prophesied that the former rains and the latter rains would be restored to Israel in the time the Messiah would appear.

Then shall we know, if we follow on to know the LORD: his going forth is prepared as the morning; and he shall come unto us as the rain, as the latter and former rain unto the earth.

—Hosea 6:3

Although 90 percent of the water needs of Israel come from the Sea of Galilee (a relatively small body of water), the sea remains full. As the population of Israel has increased, so too has the average rainfall.

The reason the Sea of Galilee has remained so unpolluted over the thousands of years is due to Lake Huleh. Lake Huleh is actually a swamp. The Jordan River is fed by three tributaries, the Dan being the largest. The waters flow into the swamp of Lake Huleh about five miles north of the Sea of Galilee. As the Jordan slowly filters through the swamp, silt is removed and bacterial action purifies the water. Engineers in Israel decided they could dry up the swamp and use it for farmland, which afterward did produce good crops. However, they soon found out that God knew what He was doing when He put the swamp above the Sea of Galilee. When Huleh Lake was dried up and water from the Jordan River went directly into the Sea of Galilee, silt, muddy water, and pollution became a problem. Also, there was an explosion of the rat population in the Huleh lakebed. So at least part of the Huleh Lake swamp was restored. It is indeed miraculous how the ecology of upper Galilee provides lifesaving waters for the new nation of Israel.

This does not mean that Israel does not have a water problem, as the need for additional water increases and especially in the years when the former rains are late. However, God has promised to supply this need and He will.

The Miracle of Irrigation

To help save water for expanding agriculture, Israel's scientists came up with the computerized drip irrigation method that makes possible the growing of vegetables and fruits that have never grown in Israel before.

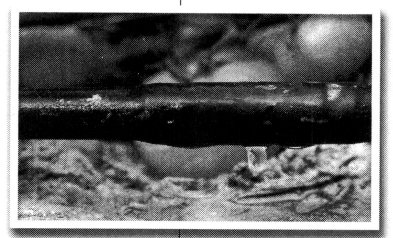

Drip irrigation was invented in 1965 in Israel because there was a limited water supply.

In this chapter on signs in Israel today, we will consider the messianic sign of irrigation. Concerning God's blessing on the land when the Jews return, we mentioned the many fruits and vegetables now grown on farms that were desert just a few years ago. One vegetable item that was not grown in Israel until recently was the avocado. Avocados have always been foreign to the Middle East. My frequent Israeli guide, Gilla Treibich, observed:

"Avocados grow on trees that are native to Central America. When the Jews came and reclaimed the land, they tried growing again the fruits and vegetables that were grown in other countries. Avocados seemed to agriculture experts a very viable and nutritious fruit, or vegetable as some thought of it. So Jewish fruit growers went to America and brought back with them avocado seedling plants. There were several varieties of avocados, so the two that were best suited were chosen for the orchards. At first the Jewish people did not take to avocados with any great relish, so how to market them? The United States had plenty of avocados, and so did New Zealand and Australia. But Europe had no avocados, and most Europeans had never eaten them. So chefs from Israel would go to France, Germany, and other European countries, and teach Europeans how to prepare and serve this very good, nourishing food. Europeans now think the avocado is the best fruit or vegetable under the sun, and Israel is only too happy to provide them."

I was amazed to see how much larger the avocado trees in Israel are compared with those in the United States or Central America. Also, the avocados grown in Israel are much larger, and this is just another example of the messianic sign of this tiny nation filling the earth with fruit.

Of course, the tremendous crops of fruits and vegetables in Israel would not be possible without irrigation, and Israel has the best and most efficient system in the world. Also, even irrigation in Israel fulfills a messianic prophecy.

> In that day will I raise up the tabernacle of David that is fallen, and close up the breaches thereof; and I will raise up his ruins, and I will build it as in the days of old:... Behold, the days come, saith the LORD, that the plowman shall overtake the reaper, and the treader of grapes him that soweth seed; and the mountains shall drop sweet wine, and all the hills shall melt.... And I will plant them upon their land, and they shall no more be pulled up out of their land which I have given them, saith the LORD thy God.
>
> —Amos 9:11, 13, 15

In this prophecy we see again that certain developments on the land are to be considered a sign that the restoration of the kingdom of Israel and the closing of the gap between God and His earthly people is at hand. This sign means of course that Jews must be back in the land. But Amos said that something would be taking place on the land that had never happened before. Some would be preparing the land for planting on one side of the field; some would be gathering the harvest in the middle of the field; and some would be planting on the far side of the field. Amos clearly described crop rotation. The rainy seasons in Israel are from the middle of November until April. Six months out of the year the weather is hot and dry in Israel. Without irrigation this prophecy could not be fulfilled. Because the land is so rich and God has blessed it, farmers in Israel now grow three crops a year. Such a thing has never been possible before. It is an important sign that the Messianic Age is near; which means also that the translation of the church at the Rapture must be even nearer.

Sign Number 31

From Desolation to Abundant Productivity

The prophetic history of Israel that God gave to Moses is in itself proof that the Bible is the infallible, inspired Word of God. In Deuteronomy 28:1-6 Moses tells Israel that God has given them a good land that He has blessed so that it will produce an abundance of fruit, cattle, sheep, and crops. The condition of this blessing from God was that they would obey the Lord and His commandments. But God also revealed to Moses that times would come when they would not obey the Law, and the consequence of Israel's sins is described in Deuteronomy 28:15–18:

> But it shall come to pass, if thou wilt not hearken unto the voice of the LORD thy God, to observe to do all his commandments and his statutes which I command thee this day; that all these curses shall come upon thee, and overtake thee: Cursed shalt thou be in the city, and cursed shalt thou be in the field. Cursed shall be thy basket and thy store. Cursed

shall be the fruit of thy body, and the fruit of thy land, the increase of
thy kine, and the flocks of thy sheep.

In Deuteronomy 28:52–62 Moses foretells the Roman occupation of
the land and the siege of Jerusalem when the Israelites would become
so hungry they would "eat the fruit of thine own body, the flesh of thy
sons and of thy daughters, which the LORD thy God hath given thee, in
the siege, and in the straitness, wherewith thine enemies shall distress
thee" (Deuteronomy 28:53). When the Romans laid siege to Jerusalem
in A.D. 70 at the time of the Passover and trapped a million Jews within
the walls, food became so scarce over the ensuing months that many
ate their own children. The complete account of this awful time is fully
described in Josephus. And then in the concluding verses of the chapter
Moses described the scattering of the Jews into all nations. In chapter
twenty-nine of Deuteronomy Moses describes the result of God's curse
on the land during the Diaspora:

> And that the whole land thereof is brimstone, and salt, and burning,
> that it is not sown, nor beareth, nor any grass groweth therein, like
> the overthrow of Sodom, and Gomorrah . . . which the LORD overthrew
> in his anger, and in his wrath: Even all nations shall say, Wherefore
> hath the LORD done thus unto this land? what meaneth the heat of
> this great anger? Then men shall say, Because they have forsaken the
> covenant of the LORD God of their fathers, which he made with them
> when he brought them forth out of the land of Egypt: For they went
> and served other gods . . . And the anger of the LORD was kindled
> against this land. . . .
>
> —Deuteronomy 29:23–27

It was very evident that every prophecy relating to the future of Israel
from the time of Moses had been fulfilled to this date. Hosea, Amos,
Isaiah, Jeremiah, Ezekiel, and most of the other minor prophets confirm
and support the prophecy of Moses. The entire context of prophecy in
the Old Testament, which is also confirmed in the New Testament, presents the futuristic schedule for Israel. When the Jew is absent from the
land, as Moses said, the land is cursed and will not grow even enough
grass for sheep. When the Jews come back to the land, God blesses it
again, and the land produces its full increase as the Lord has promised:

> Thou shalt no more be termed Forsaken; neither shall thy land any
> more be termed Desolate: but thou shalt be called Hephzibah [my

delight], and thy land Beulah [wife]: for the LORD delighteth in thee, and thy land shall be married.

—Isaiah 62:4

He shall cause them that come of Jacob to take root: Israel shall blossom and bud, and fill the face of the world with fruit.

—Isaiah 27:6

It is almost beyond belief the amount of fruit, vegetables, and nuts this rocky land produces today. Every kind fruit or vegetable known to man grows in Israel with the exception of the coconut.

Mark Twain visited Israel in 1867, which would have been about twenty years before Jews began returning, and below is an excerpt from his description of the land from his book, *Innocents Abroad:*

Israeli field worker

> There is not a solitary village throughout its whole extent [valley of Jezreel]—not for thirty miles in either direction. . . . One may ride ten miles hereabouts and not see ten human beings. . . . For the sort of solitude to make one dreary, come to Galilee. . . . Nazareth is forlorn. . . . Jericho lies a mouldering ruin. . . . Bethlehem and Bethany, in their poverty and humiliation . . . untenanted by any living creature. . . . A desolate country whose soil is rich enough, but is given over wholly to weeds, . . . a silent, mournful expanse, . . . a desolation. . . . We never saw a human being on the whole route. . . . Hardly a tree or shrub anywhere. Even the olive trees and the cactus, those fast friends of a worthless soil had almost deserted the country. . . . Of all the lands there are for dismal scenery, Palestine must be the prince. The hills barren and dull, the valleys unsightly deserts [inhabited by] swarms of beggars with ghastly sores and malformations. Palestine sits in sackcloth and ashes . . . desolate and unlovely. . . .

There is a misconception propagated in the news media that the returning Jews have robbed the Palestinians of their land and farms and cities. Nothing could be further from the truth. Only when the Jews began to develop the land, establish farms, water systems, roads, and cities did the wandering Palestinians and Islamic bedouin tribes come into Israel to profit from the work the Jews had done. Now the Islamic nations want the Jews to leave and go back to the nations they immigrated from. After 1973, Israel took possession of about half the Sinai Desert between the western border and the Nile River. They began to build cities and develop gardens and orchards in the desert. President Carter negotiated a treaty whereby Israel gave the land back. Today the entire area has gone back to desert.

When Israel is in the land, the land produces and fills the world with fruit; when Israel is absent from the land, it becomes a desert. This is visible evidence that the land belongs to Israel. It is also proof, as the Bible declares, that God will never take the land from them again. Whatever the political problems that exist today, Jesus will take care of it when He comes (Zechariah 14:16–21). The continuing controversy between Israel and the nations of the world indicates again that this is the last generation and the troubles in the time that never was or ever will be again may be just around the corner. This means also that every Christian should be making every effort to bring their loved ones into the ark of safety, which is salvation by faith in Jesus Christ.

Sign Number 32

The Pre–Tribulation Israeli Wars

Why do the heathen rage, and the people imagine a vain thing? The kings of the earth set themselves, and the rulers take counsel together, against the LORD, and against his anointed, saying, Let us break their bands asunder, and cast away their cords from us. He that sitteth in the heavens shall laugh: the Lord shall have them in derision. Then shall he speak unto them in his wrath, and vex them in his sore displeasure.

—Psalm 2:1–5

In reviewing the news media minutes of the Cairo Conference of 1943, the Tehran Conference of one month later in 1943, the Yalta Conference of February 1945, and the Potsdam Conference of July 1945, I was unable to discover any consideration by the Allied world leaders of the plight of the Jews in Europe or the establishment of a Jewish State. It appears that God took matters, though, and fulfilled the prophecy of Zechariah that the death of three great world leaders in one month would signal the return of the Jews in the last days (Zechariah 11:8), and a few verses later in Zechariah 12:3 we read, "And in that day

will I make Jerusalem a burdensome stone for all people. . . ."

On April 12, 1945, President Roosevelt died; on April 28, 1945, Mussolini was killed by insurgents; and on April 30, 1945, Adolf Hitler committed suicide. Between the death of three world leaders and the return of the Jews, the prophet indicated that Israel would endure a series of wars until the Messiah came: "In that day will I make the governors of Judah like an hearth of fire among the wood, and like a torch of fire in a sheaf; and they shall devour all the people round about, on the right hand and on the left . . ." (Zechariah 12:6).

1. This prophecy cannot refer to wars involving Israel prior to 1948. We note again that Israel, when these wars occur, will be ruled by governors, not a king or a prince. After the return of the remnant from Babylon, Israel remained militarily weak, dominated by Persia, Greece, Syria, Egypt, and Rome. Also, this prophecy could not refer to the A.D. 66–70 Jewish rebellion against Rome. Israel was the nation devoured, not all the people on the left and the right.
2. This could not be a reference to wars during the Kingdom Age, because all the weapons of war will be destroyed and there will be peace for one thousand years.
3. These wars prophesied by Zechariah had to occur between 1948 and the coming of the Messiah, and several of these wars have already happened exactly as the prophet foretold.

The overwhelming victories of tiny Israel over vastly superior armies of Egypt (on the left hand) and Syria and Jordan (on the right hand) in 1948, 1967, and 1973, amazed the entire world. In addition to the exceptions noted above, Zechariah in this prophecy could not be referring to Armageddon. At the time of Armageddon only one–third of the Jews who had been living in the land will be left alive, and these will be hiding in a place of refuge, which the Bible indicates will be Petra.

War of 1948: The day after David Ben Gurion declared Israel to be an independent nation on May 14, 1948, Egyptian airplanes bombed Tel Aviv. Within the week, the combined armies of Lebanon, Syria, and Iraq moved to take over the cities of the north and in the Galilee area. Experienced and battle–tested Arab forces armed by England moved across the Jordan to Jericho to occupy Bethlehem and Jerusalem. In the meantime, a large Egyptian army moved across the Sinai to occupy Gaza and take Tel Aviv. There appeared to be no way the poorly trained and equipped Jewish fighters could withstand the might of a combined army of five Arab states. General George Marshall warned Ben Gurion that the Israeli forces would be liquidated within seventy–two hours, but miraculously, Israel won, astounding world military experts. The Independence War lasted about six months.

1967 Six–Day War: Although a U.N.–arranged armistice ended the battles between Israel and the Arab alliance, the war continued on a terrorist and guerrilla basis. Between 1951 and 1955, nine hundred sixty–seven Israelis (men, women, and children) were killed in these types of attacks. In 1956 there was a brief period of hostilities involving Israeli, French, and British forces when Nasser of Egypt took sole possession of the Suez Canal. Between 1956 and 1966 terrorist attacks—the artillery shelling by the Syrians of northern Israel from high mountains on the Golan Heights—continued. The Soviet Union, attempting to put more pressure on the United States in the Middle East, heavily armed the Arab nations from Morocco to Iran, and goaded the Arab alliance to destroy Israel in a final gigantic war. Between May 30 and June 4, 1967, the combined armed forces of Egypt, Iraq, Jordan, Saudi Arabia, Kuwait, Algeria, and Lebanon invaded Israel. The tiny nation of Israel responded once more and within six days had conquered the Sinai, Golans, West Bank, and East Jerusalem, recalling the prophecy of Zechariah that in that day the weakest Jew would be stronger than King David.

Israeli soldiers at the Western Wall after the Six–Day War in 1967

Yom Kippur War: The Arab mind–set accepts the historic Hannah–Elizabeth position that patience and stubbornness in the end will win out. The Arabs can afford to lose ninety–nine wars—all they have to do is win the one hundredth war. Israel cannot afford to lose even one war. After the Six–Day War of 1967, the Arab nations, with Russian help, simply began to arm for the next round. October 6, 1973, was not only a Jewish sabbath, it was Yom Kippur, the most holy day in Israel. No Jew is supposed to work, eat, travel, listen to the radio, or watch television on this day. The Arabs took advantage of this knowledge about Jewish religious worship. So on this day, without warning, Egypt and Syria attacked Israel with one thousand airplanes, four thousand tanks, and eight hundred thousand men. To this force Saudi Arabia, Kuwait, and Jordan added more tanks, men, and planes. Because a large part of the Israeli army was on leave during Yom Kippur, and Israelis were not even watching television, it was difficult to marshal the nation's armed forces to defend against this overwhelming assault. When Israel finally got their defense forces to the battle fronts, the nation faced this monstrous army with only five hundred planes, seventeen hundred tanks, and three hundred thousand soldiers. Again, within two weeks,

the bulk of the Arab armies were destroyed or in retreat. The Israeli armed forces could have taken Damascus or Cairo at will. Russia again threatened nuclear war, and another armistice was signed.

The Camp David Agreement arranged by President Jimmy Carter in 1978 returned the Sinai to Egypt in exchange for a peace treaty between Israel and Egypt. The Oslo Accord in 1993, while resulting in a peace treaty between Israel and Jordan, has created an impossible situation that can only be terminated at the Battle of Armageddon.

Although in the 1967 Six–Day War Israel retook East Jerusalem, the Jerusalem of the Bible, and Jerusalem was inhabited again in its own place, Daniel prophesied that wars in Israel would continue until the Messiah would come, and so they have.

The 1982 war that involved Israel destroying thousands of tons of foreign military equipment and ammunition was followed by continual Arab proxy attacks by terrorists from Hezbollah, the PLO, and Hamas units. President Bill Clinton arranged an agreement whereby taxpayers of the United States moved Israeli farmers out of the Gaza Strip at a cost of over $40 billion and let the Palestinians take over the farms and greenhouses. The Palestinians promptly tore down the greenhouses and installed rocket launchers. Then, in 2007, they rained down some forty thousand rockets and missiles from Gaza and Lebanon on Israeli cities.

In 2010 the United Nations and the U.S. Obama administration continue to believe that peace between Israel and the Muslim world can be attained by Israel ceding more land or giving up East Jerusalem to be the capitol of the Palestinian State. But no peace agreement has been kept by the Palestinians because the problem is not land but the Jew back in the Middle East. Below is just a partial list of agreements, and these do not include the Gaza agreements of the past ten years:

»   The Balfour Declaration—November 2, 1917

» The Mandate for Palestine—July 24, 1922

» U.N. General Assembly Resolution 181—November 29, 1947

» Declaration of the Establishment of the State of Israel—May 14, 1948

» Protection of Holy Places Law—June 27, 1967

» The Khartoum Resolutions—September 1, 1967

» U.N. Security Council Resolution 242—November 22, 1967

» U.N. Security Council Resolution 338—October 22, 1973

» Separation of Forces Agreement between Israel and Syria—May 31, 1974

» U.N. Security Council Resolution 425—March 19, 1978

» Camp David Accord—September 17, 1978

» Peace treaty between Israel and Egypt—March 26, 1979

» Basic law: Jerusalem, capital of Israel—July 30, 1980

» Golan Heights Law—December 14, 1981

» Israel's Peace Initiative—May 14, 1989

» Madrid Peace Conference—October 30, 1991

» Israel–PLO Recognition—September 9, 1993

» Israel–Palestinian Declaration of Principles—September 13, 1993 (Oslo Accord)

» Israel–Jordan Common Agenda—September 14, 1993

» Agreement on Gaza Strip and Jericho—May 4, 1994

» Washington Declaration (Israel–Jordan–U.S.)—July 25, 1994

» Agreement on Transfer of Powers (Israel–PLO)—August 25, 1994

» Peace treaty between Israel and Jordan—October 26, 1994

» Interim agreement between Israel and Palestinians—September 28, 1995

Former Israeli prime minister Yitzhak Rabin and Palestine Liberation Organization chairman Yasser Arafat shake hands after signing a peace accord on the South Lawn of the White House, as President Clinton watches.

Who Is To Blame?

In A.D. 70 Jerusalem was destroyed and most of the Jews were either killed or sold as slaves, as already noted. Later, in A.D. 132–135, in the Bar Kochba Revolt, most of the remaining Jewish population was either killed or driven into other nations. The traditional enemies of Israel, the Edomites, descendants of Esau, took over the country. However, according to history and the Bible, the land that was known as Israel in Bible times belongs to the descendants of Abraham, the Jewish people. The Balfour Declaration of 1917 gave the Jewish people not only the right to the historical land of Israel, but also Jordan, which included the extent of the Israeli nation during the reign of King David. Nevertheless, Winston Churchill, after World War One, was instrumental in giving Jordan to the Arab tribes that fought under Lawrence of Arabia in World War One. Subsequent United Nations manipulations took almost half of the original Israel and gave it to the Palestinians, who never settled the land, and as Mark Twain and others testified, before A.D. 1900 it was unoccupied territory and practically a wasteland.

World War One was supposedly fought to make the world safe for democracy, and even today our president will make a pretense of pursuing political expedience under the guise of aiding democracies. Needless to say that in the Middle East our nation enters into political fellowship with some of the most brutal dictators who ever lived. But Israel, in fact, is the only democracy in the Middle East. We read in Zechariah 12:5–6:

> And the governors of Judah shall say in their heart, The inhabitants of Jerusalem shall be my strength in the LORD of hosts their God. In that day will I make the governors of Judah like an hearth of fire among the wood, and like a torch of fire in a sheaf; and they shall devour all the people round about, on the right hand and on the left: and Jerusalem shall be inhabited again in her own place, even in Jerusalem.

Preterists may say that this prophecy was fulfilled in A.D. 70. However, we read in the same chapter, verse 8, that God would save the feeble in that day because even a feeble person will be as strong as David. This certainly was not true in A.D. 70, as Josephus tells us that the feeble and elderly who survived the siege were all killed by Titus. Only the young and strong were kept alive.

We notice that Zechariah referred to the governors of Judah in that day. According to Hosea and other prophets, it was foretold that Israel would abide many days without a king or a prince. Isaiah had prophesied that the kings of Israel would be killed and the royal princes would be made eunuchs. The great King of Kings, the Messiah, would be born of the seed of woman as prophesied in Genesis 3:15. Jesus Christ claimed that He was the Messiah, born of a virgin, conceived by the Holy Spirit, but Israel rejected Him. The Romans appointed puppet kings of the lineage of Esau over Israel, but there was no true prince or king from the lineage of David.

The first government of Israel was a "judicial theocracy" composed of judges who governed by the Law of Moses. The second government was a "monarchy theocracy," a ruler anointed by the high priest to reign according to God's ordinances for human government.

After a remnant returned from the Babylonian captivity there was no king, so the government was evidently fashioned after the Persian government which had a representative from each of the one hundred twenty provinces. The returning Jews formed what was called the "Great Assembly" with one hundred twenty members. *Knesset* means assembly.

When Israel became a nation on May 14, 1948, a provisional state council was formed to function until the Great Assembly or Knesset members could be elected. In 1949 one hundred twenty Knesset members were elected by the citizens of Israel. The first Knesset, which was composed of multiracial representatives (including representatives of the Yemenite Jews who were returning), dealt with such issues as health, industrialization, jobs, schools, and immigration. The United Nations also delivered a referendum to the Knesset to internationalize Jerusalem, and in a speech before the Knesset on December 5, 1949, Israeli prime minister David Ben Gurion declared: "Jewish Jerusalem is an integral and inseparable part of the State of Israel, just as it is an inseparable part of the history of Israel, the faith of Israel, and the spirit of our people."

The prophet Zechariah foretold that when the Jews returned that the nation of Israel would be ruled by governors, indicating a democracy. Israel is today a democracy within a republic framework; in fact, Israel, as we have noted, is the only democratic government in all that area of the world.

As the international political sphere moves toward a new world order under a single authority, a democratic nation in the Middle East is one piece of the puzzle that doesn't fit. Therefore, we see the United Nations and its multiple affiliates evidently do not favor a strong nuclear democracy in the Middle East. However, God will decide the outcome that He has already decided, as we read in the second Psalm. The scenario being played out as affecting Israel is a prophetic warning to be ready for the coming of the Lord.

Sign Number 33

Restoration of Temple Worship

The Tabernacle served as a place of communication, worship, and sacrifice with God for Israel during the period of wandering in the wilderness and the time of the judges. King David envisioned a permanent temple to replace the tabernacle (2 Samuel 7:1–2). Because David was a man of war, he was not permitted to build the temple, but he did purchase a site for it from Araunah, the Jebusite. The temple was constructed by Solomon and dedicated as the "house of the Lord" (2 Chronicles 3:1).

Solomon's temple stood for four hundred sixteen years before it was plundered and burned by the Babylonians in 586 B.C. on the ninth day of Av. After the Babylonian captivity period ended, a returning Jewish remnant under the leadership of Zerubbabel completed the rebuilding of the temple in 515 B.C. Because Zerubbabel did not have the funds and skilled workmen available to him as Solomon did, the second temple was inferior in beauty and workmanship. However, Zerubbabel's temple was refurbished and enlarged by King Herod. The second temple was burned by the Romans on the ninth day of Av in A.D. 70.

There is a difference of opinion among orthodox and/or observing Jews whether the temple must be rebuilt before the Messiah comes. Ezekiel 40–44 relates to the building of the millennial temple, or messianic temple, so there will be such a temple. The prophet Zechariah foretold that the Messiah will build this temple:

> ... Behold the man whose name is The BRANCH; and he shall grow up out of his place, and he shall build the temple of the LORD: Even he shall build the temple of the LORD; and he shall bear the glory, and shall sit and rule upon his throne; and he shall be a priest upon his throne: and the counsel of peace shall be between them both.
>
> —Zechariah 6:12–13

According to Malachi 3:1, the Lord of the covenant with Israel will suddenly come to His temple. Jesus proposed that He was not only "The BRANCH," He was the Vine (John 15:5). Jesus also suddenly came to the temple and in rage threw out the money changers. He also, according to the Gospels, made the blind to see, the deaf to hear, and the lame to leap as a deer. He fulfilled these promised messianic miracles in type according to Paul in order to prove His claim to Israel as the Messiah: "Now I say that Jesus Christ was a minister of the circumcision for the truth of God, to confirm the promises made unto the fathers" (Romans 15:8).

We present this basic foundational information to present the evidence that Jesus Christ never confirmed a covenant with Israel. Some in Israel did believe that He was the Christ, but most did not. Jesus was rejected. This leaves us with the proposition that a false messiah must come and confirm the covenant with Israel, and after three and a half years repudiate his confirmation and stop the sacrifice and oblation:

> And he shall confirm the covenant with many for one week: and in the midst of the week he shall cause the sacrifice and the oblation to cease, and for the overspreading of abominations he shall make *it* desolate, even until the consummation, and that determined shall be poured upon the desolate.
>
> —Daniel 9:27

The pronoun "it" is in italics, meaning that this evil person will simply make desolations on earth.

> And arms shall stand on his part, and they shall pollute the sanctuary of strength, and shall take away the daily sacrifice, and they shall place the abomination that maketh desolate.
>
> —Daniel 11:31

And from the time that the daily sacrifice shall be taken away, and the abomination that maketh desolate set up, there shall be a thousand two hundred and ninety days.

—Daniel 12:11

When ye therefore shall see the abomination of desolation, spoken of by Daniel the prophet, stand in the holy place, (whoso readeth, let him understand:).

—Matthew 24:15

Let no man deceive you by any means: for that day shall not come, except there come a falling away first, and that man of sin be revealed, the son of perdition; Who opposeth and exalteth himself above all that is called God, or that is worshipped; so that he as God sitteth in the temple of God, shewing himself that he is God.

—2 Thessalonians 2:3–4

Considering every prophecy relating to the "abomination of desolation" in the temple, this awful sin will be enacted at the halfway mark of the Tribulation in a temple structure on the Temple Mount. The act constitutes a satanically possessed dictator who stands in the temple declaring to the entire world that he is the Messiah (Christ), and demanding that all nations worship him as God (Revelation 13). A period of international desolation descriptive of nuclear warfare ensues. Related scriptures foretell the destruction of Damascus, Iraq, and many other nations, including Egypt, being so contaminated that no animal can live on the land for forty years. Many other world desolations are prophesied for this time in the book of Revelation.

Some have suggested that a tabernacle could be placed in front of the Western Wall to fulfill this prophecy, but in Amos 9:14 and Acts 15:16 where the tabernacle is mentioned, the Messiah in Amos, and Jesus Christ in Acts, are indicated as builders of the tabernacle. Therefore, the tabernacle in these scriptures seems to refer to the Davidic throne and theocratic government, not a literal structure.

However, evidence would substantiate the conclusion that there must be a temple on the Temple Mount for the false messiah, or the

Cohens and Levites are being schooled to resume temple worship.

Antichrist, to desecrate. This building doubtless will be destroyed, possibly at the Battle of Armageddon. Nevertheless, there is increasing sentiment in Israel today to go ahead and make preparations for rebuilding the temple, even though Muslim guards are still in control of the Temple Mount. The Temple Institute in Jerusalem has prepared the vessels needed in temple worship, and the trumpets to welcome the Messiah. Cohens and Levites are being schooled to resume temple worship, and many observing Jews have been excited about the appearance of a red heifer that would fulfill requirements in Numbers 19 for resuming temple services. Most orthodox and observing Jews believe that the nation of Israel cannot be completely restored until the temple, the Lord's House, is once more standing on Mount Moriah.

The Temple Institute has completed all the items needed to resume temple worship, including musical instruments, the golden candelabra, the altar of burnt offering, the priests' clothing, and the various incenses. The priests have also been DNA checked to see if they are indeed descendants of Aaron—96 percent are. The Levites have been DNA checked, and something like 82 percent are of the tribe of Levi, but on the average, only about one-third of the Jews in Israel today are 100 percent Jewish.

The Temple Institute and the Temple Mount Faithful are two of the Jewish organizations wanting to rebuild the temple now and resume temple worship. Even the *Jerusalem Post* is now carrying news favorable to rebuilding the temple. The *Post's* edition of March 29, 2010, carried a front-page article with graphics about rebuilding the temple as follows:

While tensions continue to simmer around the Temple Mount after riots in and around the capital's Old City earlier this month, a new campaign calling for the construction of the Third Temple atop the holy site has made its way to the sides of 200 Egged buses in the city, which now sport posters featuring a picture of a rebuilt temple on the Mount, and nothing else.

The posters, which contain the phrase, "May the Bais Hamikdosh be rebuilt speedily and within our days," were sponsored by the Our Land of Israel group, which is led by Rabbi Shalom Dov Volpo and activist Baruch Marzel, leave out the site's current structures—namely the the Aksa Mosque and the Dome of the Rock.

The campaign's organizers chose to plaster the posters on buses whose routes take them through predominately Arab neighborhoods of east Jerusalem.

With regards to the campaign, Volpo said Israel is waiting breathlessly for the coming of the messiah and the rebuilding of the temple.

"The Arabs and President Obama know that the Temple will be built on the Temple Mount," he said. "Instead of the temporary buildings that are there today."

Speaking to *The Jerusalem Post* on Sunday, Marzel said it was no mistake that the Islamic shrines were left out of the picture.

"We're representing the truth, in front of everyone, and saying out loud what every Jew believes," Marzel said. "That the Third Temple needs to be built immediately on the Temple Mount and that the mosque should not be there."

"When we reach the end of the Pessah Seder tomorrow night, he continued, "we'll say, 'Next year in a rebuilt Jerusalem.' What does 'rebuilt' mean? It means with the Third Temple intact."

Marzel brushed off the furor the ads might elicit from the capital's Muslims, saying, "It upsets them that we're alive, and that we're living here."

We know the following from Scripture and current news reports:

1. The Antichrist will make a covenant (treaty) with Israel for one week (Daniel 9:27). A new comprehensive treaty engineered by the Obama administration could come at any time.
2. The temple will be rebuilt at some location, perhaps the Temple Mount, and temple worship resumed, because the Antichrist will break the treaty after three and a half years and cause temple worship to cease (Daniel 9:27).
3. The Antichrist will divide Israel into two nations, and it is suggested by Hillary Clinton, our present secretary of state, that East Jerusalem (the original Jerusalem) be made the capitol of the new Palestinian State (Daniel 11:39).

The restoration of temple worship is the most significant sign today that the Antichrist is probably alive right now and all the unsaved alive right now could go into the Tribulation period.

Sign Number 34

The Ashes of the Red Heifer

In 1981 I did a series of programs with Dr. Emil Gaverluk relating to the "ashes of the red heifer." One of the Dead Sea Scrolls, the Copper Scroll, states: "On the way from Jericho to Succakah, by the River Ha Kippa, in the tomb of Zadok the priest, which is the cave that has two openings. On the opening on the side of the north [the view is toward the east dig] two and one–half cubits under the plaster and there will be found the *kallal* and under it one book."

The *kallal* was the container of the ashes of the last, or ninth, red heifer. The *kallal* was a pot made of cow dung and clay. Other sources indicate the *kallal* was a stone pot. According to Rabbi Chaim Richman, the ashes of the red heifer were divided into three parts: (1) One part was in the temple to be used for purification; (2) one in the women's court to be saved as a memorial; and (3) one at the place of burning for purification of the priests at the next burning (*Mystery of the Red Heifer*, p. 41). It is also assumed that the remains of the third portion would be put into the ashes of the subsequent red heifer to purify them—just in case they were not as pure as they should be.

The consensus in 1981 was that the ashes of the last red heifer must be found in order to purify the ashes of the next red heifer. However, most ceremonial and dietary laws have been amended and enlarged by opinion

and tradition in Judaism over the past three thousand years, much as the Roman Catholic Church has amended doctrines and liturgy through encyclicals and papal decrees. Instructions in Numbers 19 for the particulars of the red heifer sacrifice don't mention the need for including the ashes of the previous heifer in the ashes of the succeeding heifer. Although it is thought by some Jews that the Messiah will come when the tenth red heifer is sacrificed, this cannot be documented by Scripture.

In 1981 when we began to bring information to light regarding the necessity of finding the ashes of the last red heifer that were either on the Temple Mount, or the "place of burning" on Mount Olivet, what response we received was, for the most part, negative and critical. The majority of Christians and Jews had no idea what we were talking about, and those who did felt it didn't make any difference anyway. However, in 1997 the entire world was talking about the red heifer. Why?

The so-called Oslo Agreement has brought Israel to an impasse. The West Bank for a Palestinian State has been created, but as predicted by some, it is a base for terrorists, and an instigation of unrest and hatred against Israel. Even so, there are still over 1 million Arabs (or Muslims) living in Israel proper, with daily demands against the political security of Jerusalem and the Jewish settlements. From an Orthodox point of view, the only hope is the coming of the Messiah, just as Josephus reported He was the last hope of the Jews in A.D. 70. The growing aspiration of many religious Jews is to help the Messiah to come sooner by rebuilding the temple. In order to initiate restored temple worship, there must be the ashes of a pure red heifer. Therefore, there is no need to rebuild the temple until such ashes are in evidence. Quoting from *The Mystery of the Red Heifer* (p. 8), by Rabbi Richman:

> What does a red heifer have to do with any of this? Perhaps it would be difficult for some to believe that a cow could be so important. But the truth, the fate of the entire world depends on the red heifer. For God has ordained that its ashes alone is the single missing ingredient for the reinstatement of biblical purity—and thereafter, the rebuilding of the Holy Temple.

It is thought by some that before the temple was destroyed in A.D. 70, that Essenes took vessels and items required for temple worship, either before or after it was destroyed, and hid them in sixty–seven places. If there were three *kallals* of ashes, then it is possible that one may still be buried under the Temple Mount, or hidden near the "place of burning" on Mount Olivet.

The ordinance of the Law commanding the sacrifice of a red heifer is found in Numbers 19:1–2: "And the LORD spake unto Moses and unto Aaron, saying, This is the ordinance of the Law which the LORD hath commanded, saying, Speak unto the children of Israel, that they bring thee a red heifer without spot, wherein is no blemish, and upon which never came yoke."

It should be noted that this ordinance came from the Lord, by direct oral instruction from God Himself. Although this ordinance was not a part of the Ten Commandments, it was a commandment from the Lord.

This was a commandment specifically to the "children of Israel." It was never a commandment to the Gentiles.

The children of Israel were to bring a red heifer. A red heifer is simply a young red female bovine. Melody, one red heifer in Israel, was the result of artificial insemination from a bull in Sweden. Clyde Lott in Mississippi was breeding cattle for Israel trying to breed a pure red heifer. Rabbi Richman gives two incidents where the red heifer sacrificed was purchased from Gentiles, so this would be a matter for the rabbinate to decide. It is also concluded that the red heifer must be born in Israel, and although this is not directly commanded in the ordinance of the Law, it may be inferred.

Reverend Lott shared with us that it would be impossible to ship an acceptable red heifer to Israel, because it would first have to be marked with ink, and then with stapled tags in the ears, giving the record of inspection and vaccination. The Lord commanded that the red heifer be without spot or blemish. Reverend Lott hoped that one of his heifers might be shipped to Israel to give birth there to an acceptable heifer, or send impregnated eggs to be implanted in cows in Israel.

The final qualification for a red heifer to meet the Lord's requirements is that it must never have worn a yoke. Rabbi Richman contends that if someone even leaned on it, the heifer would have to be disqualified.

Sacrifices, even in paganism, signify substitutionary judgment or death to placate the gods' wrath as justification to a divine authority. Does this historical evidence negate or depreciate the sacrificial commandments by God in the Law? Not at all. In fact, the vain efforts of the heathen to justify his sins and lost condition through a substitute sacrifice only verifies the lessons in type and example under Mosaic Law.

(For when the Gentiles, which have not the law, do by nature the things contained in the law, these, having not the law, are a law unto themselves: Which shew the work of the law written in their hearts, their conscience also bearing witness, and their thoughts the mean while accusing or else excusing one another;) In the day when God shall judge the secrets of men by Jesus Christ according to my gospel.

—Romans 2:14–16

Melody, the red heifer born in Israel

Under the Law, animals were sacrificed at the Passover and Yom Kippur, and there were daily intermittent sacrifices of doves, pigeons, etc. Like the burning of the red heifer, all such sacrificial offerings in some way were to teach Israel of their need for a substitutionary eternal sacrifice, who once and for all would take away their sins (Romans 11).

Red is the color of sin: "Come now, and let us reason together, saith the LORD: though your sins be as scarlet, they shall be as white as snow; though they be red like crimson, they shall be as wool" (Isaiah 1:18).

Red is also the color of blood, and the priest sprinkled the blood of the heifer seven times before the congregation. There are at least fifty scripture references in the New Testament (check your concordance) that warn the lost that there is nothing that can erase, forgive, atone, or redeem (from or for) sin, but the blood of Jesus Christ.

The commandment that the red heifer was to do no labor signified that salvation is not of works, but by faith through God's grace (Ephesians 2:8–9).

And ye shall give her unto Eleazar the priest, that he may bring her forth without the camp, and one shall slay her before his face: And Eleazar the priest shall take of her blood with his finger, and sprinkle of her blood directly before the tabernacle of the congregation seven times: And one shall burn the heifer in his sight; her skin, and her flesh, and her blood, with her dung, shall he burn.

—Numbers 19:3–5

On the Day of Atonement the high priest entered into the Holy of Holies in the temple to present the blood of the animal, representing in type the blood of Jesus Christ which was to be offered in the fullness of time. Likewise, Eleazar the priest sprinkled the blood from the red heifer seven times before the tabernacle. Eleazar was the third son of Aaron, a type of Christ in sprinkling the blood seven times before the Ark. Seven is the number of divine perfection, and only the blood of Jesus Christ is the perfect atonement for sin. "Neither by the blood of goats and calves, but by his own blood he entered in once into the holy place, having obtained eternal redemption for us" (Hebrews 9:12).

Only a high priest could offer up blood for a sin offering, so in offering up His own blood, Jesus Christ became our eternal High Priest (Hebrews 7:21).

The burning of the red heifer as a sin offering was a type of the sinner's eternal judgment in the lake of fire. The penalty for sin was satisfied in type.

"And the priest shall take cedar wood, and hyssop, and scarlet, and cast it into the midst of the burning of the heifer" (Numbers 19.6). Hyssop is a fragrant, leafy, hairy vine plant that grows out of walls and above the ground in Israel. It was used by Moses as a symbol of purity, and it was the only plant that could be used to sprinkle the waters of purification. Scarlet is a symbol for sin, and the cedar is a representative wood for the cross. In the hyssop, cedar, and scarlet being cast into the fire as it burned the red heifer, we see a representation of Jesus Christ dying for the sins of the world:

> For he hath made him to be sin for us, who knew no sin; that we might be made the righteousness of God in him.
>
> —2 Corinthians 5:21

> And a man that is clean shall gather up the ashes of the heifer, and lay them up without the camp in a clean place, and it shall be kept for the congregation of the children of Israel for a water of separation: it is a purification for sin.
>
> —Numbers 19:9

According to the Mishna and the Talmud, it became a serious matter of contention as to which man in Israel would be clean enough to gather the ashes of the red heifer, or to draw the water for purification, so pregnant women would actually give birth to their children within the temple area. These children would never hear vulgar language, be near sinful acts, and even their feet would not touch the ground. An ox–drawn cart would carry them to the Spring of Siloam—all cleansed with the ashes of the red heifer in the waters of separation and purification. The children would never get off the cart, but would lower purified stone

Pool of Siloam

vessels into the spring by attached strings. These were the precautions that the priests and Levites would take to carry out the type that foreshadowed the salvation that the Messiah would bring.

"And he that gathereth the ashes of the heifer shall wash his clothes, and be unclean until the even: and it shall be unto the children of Israel, and unto the stranger that sojourneth among them, for a statute for ever" (Numbers 19:10). This sacrifice was a type of purification that would last forever, and not just for Israel, but for any strangers, meaning Gentiles. When the sin–bearer came to fulfill the type, Israel clung to the type and refused to accept the truth. "He came unto his own, and his own received him not. But as many as received him, to them gave he power to become the sons of God, even to them that believe on his name" (John 1:11–12).

Not only were the waters for purification (which contained a small amount of the ashes of the red heifer) used for cleansing and separation (sanctification) of the temple, vessels, furnishings, priests, Levites, and even the congregation, we read in the ordinances that any Israelites who touched a dead body, or even came into close proximity to a dead body, must be sprinkled with the waters of purification. This signified that there is no death for those who have been purified by faith in the atoning blood of Jesus Christ (1 Corinthians 15:54–57).

The water of purification containing the ashes of the red heifer for daily cleansing and sanctification was a definitive setting forth of the absolute truth of God that the blood wherewith we are saved from sin is the same blood wherewith we are daily cleansed from sins we commit either by commission or omission.

> But if we walk in the light, as he is in the light, we have fellowship one with another, and the blood of Jesus Christ his Son cleanseth us from all sin. If we say that we have no sin, we deceive ourselves, and the truth is not in us. If we confess our sins, he is faithful and just to forgive us our sins, and to cleanse us from all unrighteousness.
>
> —1 John 1:7–9

The Place of Burning

The "place of burning," Miphkad Altar, is located just below the northern summit of the Mount of Olives, on a line from the entrance to the temple through the Eastern Gate. There is now a problem in using the traditional "place of burning" to sacrifice a new red heifer. According to Ezekiel 44:1–4, the Eastern Gate, which is closed, will not be opened until the Messiah comes. Also, the "place of burning" is in the possession of the Arabs and Muslims, and a sacrificial service to make possible the rebuilding of the temple would start another holy war.

There is one popular view that Jesus Christ had to be sacrificed on the "place of burning" in order to fulfill the red heifer type and example. However, if Jesus were crucified on the Mount of Olives, the following would have to be considered:

1. Everything that Jesus did on the Mount of Olives was duly noted by the writers of the four Gospels. If Jesus were crucified on the Mount of Olives, the Gospel writers would have so stated.
2. Two others accused of serious crimes were crucified with Jesus, and the Romans would not have willfully incurred Jewish anger by executing criminals on a Jewish holy site.
3. Golgotha, the hill in the shape of a skull, is scripturally presented as the place where Jesus was crucified. This hill is just outside the city wall near the Damascus Gate—not on Mount Olivet.
4. We read in Hebrews 13:12 that Jesus shed His blood and suffered without the gate. In John 19:20 we read that Jesus was crucified "nigh" to the city, and we also read that the tomb where He was laid was "nigh" to where He was crucified. There is only one place that fits this description—Golgotha, just outside the wall, near the Damascus Gate, with a tomb of a rich man in a garden near Skull Hill.
5. The Romans always crucified victims near the well-traveled road, and the highway to the north exited from the Damascus Gate past Golgotha.

Interest by world Jewry in the red heifer manifests a growing conviction that the coming of Israel's Messiah is imminent. The *Boston Globe* of April 6, 1997, in a story titled "Heifer's Appearance in Israel Stirs Hopes, Apocalyptic Fears," relates:

> . . . a sign of the coming of the Messiah and decried as a walking atom bomb. Of a variety believed extinct for centuries, the red heifer is seen by some as the missing link needed for religious Jews to rebuild their ancient Temple in Jerusalem. Sacrificing the animal in its third year and using its ashes in a purification rite would allow Jews to return 2,000 years later to the Temple site, a spot holy to both Jews and Muslims. . . . Many fear that the calf's arrival could create an explosive situation.

The lengthy story continues to relate world concerns that growing Jewish fervor over a red heifer will "launch a war with the world's 1 billion Muslims." Meanwhile, such messianic groups in Israel as the Temple Mount Faithful, Temple Institute, and others, continue to prepare the priests and Levites to resume temple worship—while also making the vessels, furnishings, and musical instruments. According to Jesus and the prophets, someone will make possible the resuming of temple worship at a site called the Holy Place. According to orthodox Jews, this place must be on Mount Moriah. A red heifer will be sacrificed and its ashes will be sprinkled over this structure and the Cohens, but then the man who makes this possible will declare himself to be the Messiah. This abomination will trigger a worldwide conflagration of desolation (Matthew 24; Revelation 19, etc.). This person is probably in the world today.

Like all such types and messianic representations in the Bible, the sacrificial ordinance of the red heifer is an object lesson in God sending His only begotten Son, Jesus Christ, into the world to be offered for us, in our place. Only when Jesus literally returns at the Battle of Armageddon will Israel understand the true meaning of this Old Testament typology (Romans 11:25–28; Revelation 1:7; Matthew 24:15–27; Zechariah 12:10).

To Christians, news relating to a red heifer in Israel means that Jesus Christ is coming back soon, and it is near, even at the doors. To non-Christians it means to either receive Jesus Christ as Lord and Savior or get ready for a seven-year time of judgment, a time which Jesus said would be "great tribulation, such as was not since the beginning of the world to this time, no, nor ever shall be" (Matthew 24:21).

The online encyclopedia Wikipedia.com states of the red heifer:

In the Book of Daniel is a reference to a Red Heifer. In Daniel 12:10, God tells Daniel that in the last days, "many shall be purified and made white"; a reference to the purification ritual of the Red Heifer, "Though your sins be as scarlet, they shall be as white as snow" (Isa. 1:18; Num. 19:6). The analogy appears to relate to a partner of the returning End Time messiah.

Although I am a Christian, I am also an honorary member of the Temple Institute, which reported on the "Tenth Red Heifer":

From Moses to the Second Temple: Only Nine Red Heifers
The Mishna teaches that up until the destruction of the Second Temple, ashes had been prepared from a total of only nine red heif-

ers. The very first red heifer was processed by Moses himself—as the verse states, ". . . have them bring you a red heifer." The second was done by the prophet Ezra in the days of the First Temple, and during the entire era of the Second Temple only seven more heifers were used for ashes. This was enough to provide for the nation's needs for purification throughout all those years.

The names of all the High Priests who prepared those seven heifers during Second Temple times are recorded by the Mishna: Simon the Just and Yochanan each made two; El'yhoeini ben Hakof, Chanamel HaMitzri and Yishmael ben Pi'avi processed one heifer each. Thus, from the time that Moses received the commandment of the red heifer from the Holy One, blessed be He, until the destruction of the Second Temple, purifying ashes had been produced by the hands of these great leaders from a total of nine red heifers.

The Tenth Red Heifer Will be Prepared by the Messiah

In recounting this historical record in his commentary to the Mishna, the great Maimonides ends with the enigmatic statement: ". . . and the tenth red heifer will be accomplished by the king, the Messiah; may he be revealed speedily, Amen, May it be God's will."

The *National Review* in an article titled "Red Heifer Days" stated in part:

Timothy Weber, dean of Northern Baptist Theological Seminary in Lombard, Ill., has written extensively about the worldview of apocalypse-minded American Protestants. He tells NRO that "Bible teachers are foaming at the mouth over what's happening now in Israel."

"It really does play into the longstanding scenario that dispensationalists have believed would happen in the End: a growing disdain for Israel, Israel's isolation from the rest of the world, and mounting pressure on the Jewish state," Weber says. "This all leads up to the emergence of an Antichrist, who will step up and bring peace to the situation, and Israel and the world will welcome him as a solution to an apparently unsolvable problem."

. . . Put another way: You don't have to believe that a rust-colored calf could bring about the end of the world—or that 72 black-eyed virgins await the pious Islamic suicide bomber in paradise—but there are many people who do, and are prepared to act on that belief. This is a stubborn reality that eludes many of us in the modern, secular West, particularly those who work in the media, and who are therefore responsible for reporting and explaining the world to the masses.

Not only are there efforts in the United States to produce a 100 percent red heifer for Israel, there are several locations in Israel also dedicated to the same effort, one of which is a *kibbutz* about twenty–five miles north of Eilat. International anxiety by many over the sacrifice of a red heifer in Israel that will announce to the world that "the" or "a" messiah is here, is certainly one of the most unusual and remarkable signs that this is indeed the very last generation before the Lord Jesus Christ returns.

Sign Number 35

The Eastern Gate and the Dead Sea

Two Interesting Prophetic Places

In leading some fifty-three tours to Israel, the most important places to visit are, of course, the Western Wall, the Temple Mount, the Pool of Bethesda, and the Jewish, Christian, and Arab division of the Old City. The meeting points for these sites are associated with certain gates. The Jewish quarter is accessed by the Jaffa Gate; the Western Wall, and the Temple Mount by the Dung Gate; and the Garden Tomb, the Pool of Bethesda, and St. Anne's Church by the Lion Gate, also called St. Stephen's Gate, because by tradition this was where Stephen was stoned. One of the most important gates on the city walls is the Eastern Gate, also called the Golden Gate, or

Closed Eastern Gate

the Beautiful Gate. The reason that this is the most important gate is not because of in-and-out traffic, because there is none. The reason, of course, is because it is sealed and Muslim guards are stationed inside the gate to keep anyone with a bomb from blowing it open. The reason that someone would try to open it is also the reason for its importance in the past, today, and in the future.

Suleiman's walls had the following gates: Damascus Gate, Lion or Stephen's Gate, Dung Gate (Western Wall Gate), Zion Gate, and Jaffa Gate. Some archaeologists date the Eastern Gate later, but how could

Suleiman have sealed it if he did not built it. Ezekiel was a Babylonian captive, yet he wrote two thousand years before Suleiman:

> Then he brought me back the way of the gate of the outward sanctuary which looketh toward the east; and it was shut. Then said the LORD unto me; This gate shall be shut, it shall not be opened, and no man shall enter in by it; because the LORD, the God of Israel, hath entered in by it, therefore it shall be shut. It is for the prince; the prince, he shall sit in it to eat bread before the LORD; he shall enter by the way of the porch of that gate, and shall go out by the way of the same.
>
> —Ezekiel 44:1–3

The forty-fourth chapter of Ezekiel clearly gives a description of the messianic temple and the requirements for the priests to minister in this temple, which the Messiah Himself will build. The verses quoted referred to the closing of the Eastern Gate. The tourist can look over the Temple Mount from the Mount of Olives and see quite plainly that the Eastern Gate is closed.

When the remnant from the Babylonian captivity era returned to rebuild Jerusalem, the wall, and the temple, they built within the wall a gate on the east side, just on the west bank of the Brook Kidron, opposite the Garden of Gethsemane. This wall was torn down at the conclusion of the Roman siege of Jerusalem in A.D. 70. During the next fifteen hundred years various efforts were made to rebuild the wall, but then other invaders would tear the wall down. The wall with the Eastern Gate today was built by Suleiman the Magnificent in 1542 after the Ottoman Turks had conquered most of the Middle East. After the wall had been completed, Suleiman discovered that the surveyors and architects had failed to extend the wall around Mount Zion, so he had them all beheaded.

Within the last decade the Eastern Gate of the wall that the Romans destroyed was discovered a few feet below the present gate. At the time of Jesus Christ, this gate was probably also called the Beautiful Gate, or the Golden Gate. This following information is taken from page 658 of the *Zondervan Pictorial Encyclopedia of the Bible:*

> **Gate, The Beautiful.** A gate in Herod's Temple, q.v. Whereas the "Beautiful Gate" of the NT Temple is known only from Acts 3, the phrase prob. refers to that entrance way, famous for its imported Corinthian bronze doors, which was the only E gate from the surrounding Court of the Gentiles into the Court of the Women (Jos. War. V. 5. 3). It was once identified with the single E gate that led from the

Kidron Valley, through the outer wall and "Solomon's Porch," into the Court of the Gentiles—a fact that may account for the name of the later entrance way, not itself sealed up, that was built over it and called "Porta Aurea," the "Golden Gate." After Pentecost, a man lame from his mother's womb was laid daily at the Beautiful Gate to ask for alms, and was miraculously healed by Peter and John in the name of Jesus Christ (Acts 3:2, 10).

When Jesus was in Jerusalem he lodged with Mary, Martha, and Lazarus in Bethany. The obvious route from Bethany to the temple would have been over the Mount of Olives, through the Garden of Gethsemane, and entry by the Eastern Gate. Some may contend that Jesus would not have gone through this gate because it was adjacent to the Court of the Women and the Court of the Gentiles. However, it is obvious from Acts 3 that Peter and John used this gate, and up until Acts 10 Peter was careful not to defile himself with Gentile associations. Inasmuch as Jesus had fellowship with Mary and Martha, and sat down with publicans and Samaritans, it is quite probable that He would not have had an aversion to going through the Eastern Gate. We would also think that the Jewish builders of this gate would not have used such beautiful workmanship for only Gentile use.

It is not known exactly why the Eastern Gate was sealed. The explanation most often given is that Suleiman wanted better security measures imposed to keep Jews, Christians, and others considered by the Muslims as heathens, from going on the Temple Mount and "defiling" the Muslim shrine. It is also possible that Suleiman had heard of the Jewish prophecy that the Messiah would come through this gate, so he sealed it with heavy rock and concrete blocks. From Ezekiel 44:3 the subject continues to cover the worship and service of the priests and Levites who would go through the Eastern Gate into the temple after the Messiah had opened it, and we read in verse 25, "And they shall come at no dead person to defile themselves . . ." (except immediate family members). To be doubly sure, evidently, that the Messiah would not come through the Eastern Gate, the Muslims put a cemetery in front of it.

As an added further precaution that no Jew or Gentile will even get near the gate, the Jordanians have placed a Muslim guard on the inside. We have been able to tip the guard with five or ten dollars to allow us to take pictures of the inside of the gate. Nevertheless, the sealed Eastern Gate is another sign today that Israel awaits the coming of the Messianic Age.

1. Both Muslims and Jews are aware that according to Matthew and

Luke, Jesus entered the Temple Mount through the Eastern Gate. He is called the Prince, meaning a descendant of David, by both Hosea and Ezekiel.

2. Both Muslims and orthodox Jews are aware of the prophecy that the Eastern Gate will be sealed until the Messiah of Israel goes through that gate when it is opened again.

3. The Eastern Gate must also be opened at the time of the burning of the tenth red heifer, and light from the burning is to shine through the Eastern Gate, through the front door of the temple, and into the Holy of Holies. If the exact place on the Mount of Olives where the red heifer was burned could be located, the site on which the temple stood could also easily be located. This emphasizes the importance of finding the jar that holds the ashes of the ninth red heifer.

The burning of the tenth red heifer, the opening of the Eastern Gate, and the rebuilding of the temple are all three related to the appearance of Israel's Messiah. All three prophetic events are headline news today, indicating that this must indeed be the last generation before Israel's Messiah appears, whom we know as Jesus Christ at His Second Coming.

The Dead Sea

Arise, shine; for thy light is come, and the glory of the LORD is risen upon thee. . . . Gentiles shall come to thy light, . . . thy sons shall come from far. . . . Then thou shalt see . . . the abundance of the sea shall be converted unto thee, the forces of the Gentiles shall come unto thee.

—Isaiah 60:1, 3–5

In this chapter the prophet foretells the blessing of God upon Israel during the Messianic Age when the riches of the Gentiles will come to the nation, and even the abundance of the sea will be converted to them. I have often remarked to the tour members of my group that they should not complain about high prices in Israel, because they are only helping to fulfill prophecy. Many have taken Isaiah's reference to the "sea" in this scripture to mean the Dead Sea, but this is an option rather than a definitive interpretation of the text. It could refer only to the Dead Sea, but it seems a more accurate interpretation within the context would be all major oceans and seas. It is also claimed by some that the wealth of the Dead Sea is more than all the wealth of the entire world combined, but we have difficulty understanding how the wealth of the world could be computed.

It seems that the Dead Sea did not play an important role in biblical history. Amaziah killed ten thousand Edomites in the Valley of Salt at the southern end of the Dead Sea. David and his men took refuge at the canyon oasis of Ein Gedi on the western shore of the Dead Sea. Sodom and Gomorrah were evidently located on a plain that once comprised the southern half of this area.

Josephus made reference to Roman soldiers making sport of throwing prisoners from cliffs into the "Asphaltic Sea." The poor captives would think they were going to be drowned, but they would only sink a foot or two into the heavy salt and mineral waters and then bob back up to the surface. The Dead Sea was called the Asphaltic Sea at the time of Jesus because huge amounts of oil would collect and semi-solidify on the surface. Romans and Jews would take the asphalt and pitch ships. We also read in Genesis 14 that the kings of Sodom and Gomorrah and most of their armies were killed in the Vale of Siddim where there were many slime pits (bitumen, or oil pools). Hammurabi led the opposing forces, composed of the alliance of the kings of the north. There have been considerable explorations for oil in the Dead Sea area, but the Dead Sea is a part of the largest earthquake fault in the world, the Syrian–African rift, which seriously complicates drilling efforts.

The Dead Sea is so named because nothing is said to live in its waters, although in recent years a subbiological entity has been found to exist in it. A few forms of plant life around the shores of the Dead Sea have also developed a tolerance to the heavy salt and mineral water. Water in the Dead Sea has a consistency of ten–weight motor oil, and it is true that it is impossible for people to sink.

The Dead Sea is approximately fifty miles long and ten miles wide. Its principal water source is the Jordan River. Because both Israel and Jordan now use most of the water of the river, the Dead Sea water level has been lowering by approximately a foot a year. Because of the drop in the water level, a land bridge now cuts off the southern one–third of the Dead Sea, and the heavily laden mineral waters are now channeled to the Sodom mineral and potash works through a canal.

Jesus referred to the signs of His return as the days of Sodom (Luke 17:28–30). Sodom has been restored as a city; and although it is principally a community for the mineral plant works, if you were to address a letter to the postmaster of Sodom, Israel, he would get it.

The Dead Sea is the lowest place on earth, one thousand three hundred twenty feet below sea level. According to a science report taken off the Internet (www.extremescience.com/DeadSea.htm), some places in the Dead Sea are twenty–three hundred feet deep and dropping, getting twenty–three inches a year deeper. The reason for this is that the Syrian–African rift that runs through the Red Sea, through the Arava under the Dead Sea, and then northward to Syria, is getting wider by the year. Geologists are warning about a possible second volcanic eruption.

At the same time, one side of the rift is shifting to the north and the other side to the south. This could allow water from the Mediterranean Sea to run down through the Jezreel Valley to the Jordan River south of the Sea of Galilee and then into the Dead Sea.

The waters from the Dead Sea are channeled to the mineral works at Sodom to remove valuable chemicals and fertilizers. The Dead Sea is a valuable source of income to Israel, but according to Ezekiel, there will come a time when this source of income will be no more, or at least be diminished. Ezekiel wrote about the future of the Dead Sea in the Messianic Age:

> And it shall come to pass, that the fishers shall stand upon it from Engedi even unto Eneglaim; they shall be a place to spread forth nets; their fish shall be according to their kinds, as the fish of the great sea, exceeding many. But the miry places thereof and the marishes thereof shall not be healed; they shall be given to salt.
>
> —Ezekiel 47:10–11

From the land bridge across the Dead Sea near Engedi, all the way to the northern end of the Dead Sea, the waters will be as the waters of the Great Sea, or the Mediterranean Sea. Fish from the Mediterranean will come down into this section of the Dead Sea. The area south of the land bridge today evidently will remain salty. It appears that there will be a huge geological change in this area. Evidence based on the geological activity today along the Syrian–African rift would indicate another huge earthquake like the one that occurred in A.D. 749.

In the 1980s Israel planned to run a canal from the Mediterranean Sea to the Dead Sea. This would have solved the need for water to keep the Dead Sea at a constant level. This canal could also have been used for generating electricity as the water dropped almost fifteen hundred feet. Evidently the cost of such a canal was too great.

As the Dead Sea continues to drop even more than a foot a year, Israel has evidently come up with a better plan according to a *Jerusalem Post* report in April 2007. The plan calls for digging a canal from the Red Sea at Eilat into the Arava. The canal would have to be only a few feet deep, and the waters would flow downhill all the way to the Dead Sea. This is now necessary more than ever as hotels that were once on the shores of the Dead Sea are now hundreds of yards away, and the chemical works at Sodom are having trouble getting the priceless Dead Sea water. The Palestinian Authority is jubilant about the plan, and Jordan has even offered to pay for the project.

Such a plan, if completed, would fulfill the prophecy of Ezekiel. If the plan is not implemented, then the prophecy will have to wait until the coming of Messiah to be fulfilled.

While nothing prophetically is happening at these two sites, the Eastern Gate and the Dead Sea, at the time this book is going to press, the fact that both are presently in consideration of future prophetic fulfillments in the Kingdom Age, indicates that these may indeed be the last days of the last generation before Jesus returns.

Sign Number 36

Petra—A Hiding Place for Israel

In that day will I raise up the tabernacle of David that is fallen, and close up the breaches thereof; and I will raise up his ruins, and I will build it as in the days of old: That they may possess the remnant of Edom. . . .

—Amos 9:11–12

Within the context of the prophetic overview of Israel's return to the land, and the preparations of both the people and the land for the millennial Kingdom, Amos inserted a seemingly insignificant reference to the "remnant of Edom."

In the biblical record we read that Esau and Jacob were twins, but in the womb before they were born God loved Jacob and hated Esau (Romans 9:13; Malachi 1:1–3). The attitude of God toward the twin brothers was based upon what they would become and how their descendants would be included in His eternal plan and purpose. After Esau despised his birthright and traded it to Jacob, he established his kingdom in Edom. Edom comprised the southern one–third of what today is Jordan. The inhabitants of this country at the time were called Horites, and Esau chased them out of the regions of Mount Hor, or Mount Seir. *Edom* means "red" and *Seir* means "hairy," both descriptions typical of Esau's nature.

In Edom there was a rugged area, approximately

thirty–two square miles, adjacent to Mount Hor of caves and landlocked canyons, accessible only through a narrow gorge of twenty to fifty feet. The walls on either side of the narrow gorge are five to seven hundred feet high, making it difficult for invaders to capture this cavern city. It is thought that it was here that Job established his estate in the "land of Uz" (Job 1:1). It also seems evident that the apostle Paul took refuge here after his escape from Damascus. The city that became the capital of Esau's kingdom was later called Petra (rock) by the Greeks. The entire complex, including Biatra and Little Petra, comprises  an area of one hundred thirty square miles. When the descendants of Jacob were in Egypt for four hundred years, the descendants of Esau likewise multiplied in Edom. When Moses asked for permission for the children of Israel to pass through Edom on the way to the Promised Land, not only did the king of Edom refuse, but sent out an army to attack the Israelites.

The ancestral feud that existed between Esau and Jacob continued through their descendants. The biblical account of wars between Edom and Israel are numerous. However, the threat of the rising Babylonian Empire did result in a mutual assistance pact between Israel and Edom. Nevertheless, Edom betrayed Israel and actually joined Babylon in the destruction of Jerusalem and the temple:

> By the rivers of Babylon, there we sat down, yea, we wept, when we remembered Zion. We hanged our harps upon the willows in the midst thereof. For there they that carried us away captive required of us a song; and they that wasted us required of us mirth, saying, Sing us one of the songs of Zion. How shall we sing the LORD's song in a strange land? If I forget thee, O Jerusalem, let my right hand forget her cunning. If I do not remember thee, let my tongue cleave to the roof of my mouth; if I prefer not Jerusalem above my chief joy. Remember, O LORD, the children of Edom in the day of Jerusalem; who said, Rase it, rase it, even to the foundation thereof.
>
> —Psalm 137:1–7

Racial mixing was one of the ways ancient conquerors would nationally weaken occupied territories. Under the Babylonian Empire, Israelites were moved to Babylon, and Edomites were moved into Israel. Subsequently, either of their own volition or under pressure

from Babylon, the Nabateans moved into Petra. The Nabateans were descendants of Ishmael through his first son, Nabajoth. From 500 B.C. to A.D. 500 the Nabateans enlarged their territories. However, the remnant of the Edomites continued in certain areas of Edom and Israel. When the Romans moved into this area, they called the Edomites Idumæans or Edomeans (*Westminster Dictionary of the Bible,* 148). The Romans were more friendly toward the Idumæans than the Jews. The Herods were Edomite puppet rulers. It would seem that without controversy, the Palestinians of today are largely Edomite, or Idumæan, descendants. The controversy today between the Jews and the Edomites is the same as indicated in Psalm 137.

The Edomite stronghold of Petra declined in importance after the Roman Empire broke up in about A.D. 500. Many began to doubt that such a city ever existed. Finally, in 1812 a Swiss explorer visited the city and news of its antiquity and beauty was reported to the world. Shortly afterward, Jews began returning to Israel. Today various Arab interests and the United Nations are busily restoring water sources, paving roads, and making it more accessible to Jews and Gentiles alike. A Jew could not visit Petra until 1995.

The abomination of desolation initially involves an attempt to kill the Jews living in the area of Jerusalem. While Daniel describes this act specifically in his book, Jesus further added:

> When ye therefore shall see the abomination of desolation, spoken of
> by Daniel the prophet, stand in the holy place, (whoso readeth, let him
> understand:) Then let them which be in Judæa flee into the mountains
> … For then shall be great tribulation, such as was not since the begin-
> ning of the world to this time, no, nor ever shall be.
>   —Matthew 24:15–16, 21

Of this time, the prophet Isaiah indicated that a remnant of Israel would
be protected in a special place of chambers:

> Come, my people, enter thou into thy chambers, and shut thy doors
> about thee: hide thyself as it were for a little moment, until the indig-
> nation be overpast. For, behold, the LORD cometh out of his place to
> punish the inhabitants of the earth for their iniquity: the earth also
> shall disclose her blood, and shall no more cover her slain.
>   —Isaiah 26:20–21

Petra is located in the highest mountain range in the area, approximately
ten miles from the southern end of the Dead Sea. Mount Hermon is
higher, but it is over two hundred miles to the north. There are dozens
of prophetic references to a hiding place for a remnant of Israel during the "time of Jacob's trouble," also believed to be the last half of the
Tribulation period. There are many indications within these scriptures
that this hiding place will be the restored city of Petra. It appears more
than coincidental that international agencies are now busily preparing Petra for it's future. Petra was known as a place of refuge—David
found refuge here from Saul; Paul found refuge here to escape those
who sought to kill him. The following prophecy indicates this city will
be a place of refuge for Israel:

> O God, thou hast cast us off, thou hast scattered us, thou hast been
> displeased; O turn thyself to us again. . . . Who will bring me into the
> strong city? who will lead me into Edom? Wilt not thou, O God, which
> hadst cast us off? and thou, O God, which didst not go out with our
> armies? Give us help from trouble: for vain is the help of man. Through
> God we shall do valiantly: for he it is that shall tread down our enemies.
>   —Psalm 60:1, 9–12

The continuing, unsolvable controversy between the descendants of
Esau and the descendants of Jacob, along with current developments

in Petra, is another strong messianic sign in Israel today.

Amos prophesied that in the last days Israel would possess the "remnant of Edom." There must be a remnant of Edom today, and the Palestinians in Israel must be the remaining descendants of Esau.

At the conclusion of the Olivet Discourse concerning the more prominent signs in the world that would warn national populations that the Tribulation period was near, Jesus gave a separate warning to Israel in Matthew 24:15–22:

> When ye therefore shall see the abomination of desolation, spoken of by Daniel the prophet, stand in the holy place, (whoso readeth, let him understand:) Then let them which be in Judæa flee into the mountains: Let him which is on the housetop not come down to take any thing out of his house: Neither let him which is in the field return back to take his clothes. And woe unto them that are with child, and to them that give suck in those days! But pray ye that your flight be not in the winter, neither on the sabbath day: For then shall be great tribulation, such as was not since the beginning of the world to this time, no, nor ever shall be. And except those days should be shortened, there should no flesh be saved: but for the elect's sake those days shall be shortened.

When the Antichrist stands upon the Temple Mount showing himself over television to the entire world, he evidently will issue an order to kill all the Jews in the Jerusalem area, or Judæa as Jesus indicated. At that time all nations will turn against the Jews, and Israel will not have one friend in all the nations of the world. The only dependable ally of Israel since it became a nation in 1948 has been the United States, and at the writing of this chapter, our own president is letting it be known he may force Israel to accept an agreement to divide the land to make possible a Palestinian State. Daniel said the Antichrist will divide the land for gain and make a covenant with Israel for seven years, but then after three and a half years break the treaty. Jesus said at this time the Jews in Jerusalem and the surrounding area will have to immediately run for their lives, not even going into their house for a bagel or a prayer shawl. This sudden danger could be an atomic attack, or an attack suddenly by a United Nations army against a disarmed Israel. The number that will be killed and the number that will escape is given in Zechariah 13:8–9:

> And it shall come to pass, that in all the land, saith the LORD, two parts therein shall be cut off and die; but the third shall be left therein. And I will bring the third part through the fire, and will refine them

as silver is refined, and will try them as gold is tried: they shall call on my name, and I will hear them: I will say, It is my people: and they shall say, The LORD is my God.

Now, where will one-third of the Jewish population of Judæa escape to, and how will they survive for three and a half years? The answer should be obvious—Petra.

For several hundred years, from about A.D. 600 to 1810, the world doubted that Petra even existed until it was rediscovered by a Swiss explorer in 1812. Jesus said the Jews should run for the mountains, and Petra is the highest range in the area, about one hundred miles southeast of Jerusalem. When I first went to Petra, it was still a very rugged place, with one hotel; now there are seventy hotels. The roads have been improved, utilities have been installed, and it is now a United Nations Heritage Site. Also, in 2008 Petra was made one of the Seven Wonders of the World. It is a cave city with thousands of caves, lots of livestock in the area, and very rich soil with a shallow underground water table. In one area south of Petra, you can dig six feet down and get plenty of water. The soil is rich. I can remember it raining one time while I was in Petra and in a couple of days the ground was covered with blooming desert tulips.

The southern end of the Dead Sea is now a dry area due to using most of the water coming down the Jordan River for irrigation, and it is only about one hundred miles from Jerusalem straight through this area. It appears that in light of prophecy indicating that a million or more Jews will need a place of refuge for three and a half years, Petra has been especially prepared.

Many Christians have left Bibles in Petra, along with my book *Petra in History and Prophecy,* in some of the caves in this thirty square mile canyon complex. This book tells the Jews why they are in Petra and how Jesus Christ will return to lead them back to the Promised Land, as foretold by the prophet Isaiah:

Who is this that cometh from Edom, with dyed garments from Bozrah? this that is glorious in his apparel, travelling in the greatness of his strength? I that speak in righteousness, mighty to save. Wherefore art thou red in thine apparel, and thy garments like him that treadeth in the winefat? I have trodden the winepress alone; and of the people there was none with me: for I will tread them in mine anger, and trample them in my fury; and their blood shall be sprinkled upon my garments, and I will stain all my raiment. For the day of vengeance is in mine heart, and the year of my redeemed is come.

—Isaiah 63:1-4

Bozrah is approximately fifteen miles north of Petra on the old King's Highway. Its present name is el-Busaireh. The vision of Jesus Christ returning to destroy the armies of Antichrist and then lead the Jewish survivors in Petra back to Jerusalem corresponds with the vision of John in Revelation 19:11–16:

And I saw heaven opened, and behold a white horse; and he that sat upon him was called Faithful and True, and in righteousness he doth judge and make war. His eyes were as a flame of fire, and on his head were many crowns; and he had a name written, that no man knew, but he himself. And he was clothed with a vesture dipped in blood: and his name is called The Word of God. And the armies which were in heaven followed him upon white horses, clothed in fine linen, white and clean. And out of his mouth goeth a sharp sword, that with it he should smite the nations: and he shall rule them with a rod of iron: and he treadeth the winepress of the fierceness and wrath of Almighty God. And he hath on his vesture and on his thigh a name written, KING OF KINGS, AND LORD OF LORDS.

It appears obvious that Petra has been prepared just in time to serve as a hiding place for the remnant of Israel that will survive the last three and a half years of the Great Tribulation, and meet the Lord Jesus Christ as He comes for them with the greeting, "Blessed is he that cometh in the name of the Lord."

Another obvious question is, why would not the Antichrist send missiles or airplanes to destroy the Jews in Petra. On a recent tour to Petra I asked our guide why Jordan did not build an airfield in the area of Petra, as millions of tourists from all over the world were coming to see the city. He replied that there was so much magnetic and electrical activity in this mountainous area that planes did not even fly over this part of Jordan.

Also, we have to remember that the main controversy is the land of Israel and the city of Jerusalem. It probably will not be a matter of great concern to anyone that the Jews left alive in Israel are trapped in the cave city of Petra without food or ammunition. Isaiah 26:20–21 seems to reference this three and a half years in Petra:

Come, my people, enter thou into thy chambers, and shut thy doors about thee: hide thyself as it were for a little moment, until the indignation be overpast. For, behold, the LORD cometh out of his place to punish the inhabitants of the earth for their iniquity: the earth also shall disclose her blood, and shall no more cover her slain.

That God will keep His everlasting covenant with Israel is declared in many places in Scripture. The prophet Joel completed his prophecy concerning Israel with the following promise:

The LORD also shall roar out of Zion, and utter his voice from Jerusalem; and the heavens and the earth shall shake: but the LORD will be the hope of his people, and the strength of the children of Israel. So shall ye know that I am the LORD your God dwelling in Zion, my holy mountain: then shall Jerusalem be holy, and there shall no strangers pass through her any more. And it shall come to pass in that day, that the mountains shall drop down new wine, and the hills shall flow with milk, and all the rivers of Judah shall flow with waters, and a fountain shall come forth of the house of the LORD, and shall water the valley of Shittim. Egypt shall be a desolation, and Edom shall be a desolate wilderness, for the violence against the children of Judah, because they have shed innocent blood in their land. But Judah shall dwell for ever, and Jerusalem from generation to generation.

—Joel 3:16–20

The prophetic future of Israel in this last generation has been played out in great detail in newspaper headlines, magazine documentaries, and by diplomats acting out their parts at the United Nations and daily television news forums so visibly that no one of any intelligence cannot understand that Israel itself tells us these are indeed the very last days.

Part III
Terminal Apostasies

Part I of this book on irrefutable signs of the last generation concerned general worldwide signs relating to nature, scientific advancements, and social and political changes that would be evident and common knowledge. The second part was about biblical prophetic events relating to Jewish history—past, present, and future.

The third part is about four terminal apostasies that nations cannot do without coming under the terminal judgment of God: in education, teaching that there is no God (evolution); purposely transposing sodomy for natural relations between the sexes; worshipping false gods in the temple (blasphemy in the pulpits); and defiantly refusing to observe God's warning to repent.

The present international populations as well as church memberships are guilty of all four ecclesiastical transgressions beyond hope. These signs prove beyond refute that this is the terminal generation.

SIGN NUMBER 37

PUBLIC EDUCATION AND EVOLUTION

W hen I started to school on September 10, 1927, in the first grade, the school day began with a Scripture reading, prayer, and the Pledge of Allegiance. Starting school this way today can get a teacher arrested and/or fired, because it is against the law, as interpreted by the Supreme Court, but not according to our Constitution. It seems it was not unconstitutional for two hundred and twenty years, but now it is.

According to God, the teaching of children is the responsibility of the father and the mother (Deuteronomy 11:19–21). As children, George Washington, Patrick Henry, and John Adams were taught from the *New England Primer,* and even the alphabet was learned from the Bible. We publish the *New England Primer* and *Webster's Blue–Backed Speller* in one book. Following are some examples:

A wise son maketh a glad father, but a foolish son is the heaviness of his mother.

B etter is a little with the fear of the Lord, than great treasure and trouble therewith.

C ome unto Christ all ye that labor and are heavy laden and he will give you rest.

As our population increased in A.D. 1900 school boards were appointed or elected by the local citizenry to supervise the maintenance of public schools, but the local citizens were still in control. In the unionizing of labor after 1900, school teachers formed their own unions and organizations, like the NEA. The idea of educators, so-called, like John Dewey and others was to take the responsibility for teaching children away from the parents and remold the United States into a communist, socialist order. The teachers were told they were woefully underpaid and needed federal funding. In 1959 I spoke in schools in North Texas and in Oklahoma warning parents what would result from federal aid to education. The teachers won. Laws followed that took all authority from school boards and ultimately from parents. To mention God or Jesus Christ in a public school now is against the law. Our present U.S. Department of Education head is Kevin Jennings, a sodomite and the founder of Gays and Lesbians International. On a Friday in April 2010, school children were asked not to speak in school all day to show their love of and support for sodomites. In most school books, the words "mama" and "daddy" are not found.

In Romans 1 Paul warns about nations that descend to the immoral depravity of Sodom and Gomorrah, and he states a basic foundational truth in verses 19–23:

> Because that which may be known of God is manifest in them; for God hath shewed it unto them. For the invisible things of him from the creation of the world are clearly seen, being understood by the things that are made, even his eternal power and Godhead; so that they are without excuse: Because that, when they knew God, they glorified him not as God, neither were thankful; but became vain in their imaginations, and their foolish heart was darkened. Professing themselves to be wise, they became fools, And changed the glory of the uncorruptible God into an image made like to corruptible man, and to birds, and fourfooted beasts, and creeping things.

Paul as inspired of the Holy Spirit simply revealed an evident truth, that God made creeping things, birds, four-footed animals, and man. But by federal law the schools now must teach that God didn't make living things. They are taught that there was some chemical action in a mud puddle that grew into worms, then creeping things, then to birds, then to apes, and then to man. They are actually taught that there is no Creator, that there is no God. By word or inference children are taught that the idea of a Creator is a lie; your parents are just old fashioned and the Bible is a collection of myths. Therefore, they say, we simply cannot have this nonsense taught to the children, and therefore it is against the law to mention God or read the Bible in our schools.

Barna Group, an organization that keeps track of what people believe or don't believe; do or don't do; reports that 90 percent of children from Christian homes now do not ever even go to church after high school, and certainly after college. Pastors moan and groan about why their membership is declining, yet they will not say one word against evolution which is taught to our children as fact in our public school system.

In 2009 our ministry disseminated thousands of the DVD *Privileged Planet,* proving that life on earth would not be possible without a Master Creator and Sustainer. The producers were noted scientists and astronomers. In 2010 we disseminated thousands more of the DVD *Unlock the Mystery of Life.* This DVD was produced by scientists who were former evolutionists, had even written textbooks on evolution, yet now realize that they made a serious mistake and that no evolutionary process could have possibly produced DNA. Dr. Stephen Meyer in 2009 won an award for his 600-page book *The Cell* proving that life could not have evolved. Even Bill Gates, the largest computer magnate in the world, stated that DNA could not be the result of any evolutionary process because it was far more complicated than any of his computer programs. While there is a movement in scientific circles to at least consider the "theory" of Intelligent Design, all doors to the U.S. Department of Education are tightly closed to any evidence that would be contrary to the theory of evolution.

In the meantime, pro-evolution sources like the Smithsonian Institute and the federal bureaucracy have redoubled their efforts to ignore any special creation evidence and flood newsstands and television programs with so-called new geological evidence for evolution. Therefore, the ball is back in the church's court, where 99 percent of the pastors are either too stupid, lazy, or scared to play.

The May 3, 2010, edition of the *Weekly Standard* reported that a new 164-page teaching manual from President Obama's department, "White House Office of Faith-Based and Neighborhood Partnerships," proposes that churches now begin preaching a "green gospel" to promote his global warming scam program. An added carrot is held out in helping churches that have financial problems . . . and what church does not have financial problems? This lengthy article by Meghan Clyne, titled "The Green Shepherd," reads in part:

> The council hopes the new EPA faith office will also help churches and other nonprofits improve "access to financing," including "establishing revolving loan programs or working with utility companies to help finance greening building projects." The ultimate aim of all this government-supported retrofitting is clear: "Regional staff would work to engage local faith- and community-based groups to help meet Obama administration targets for greening buildings and promoting environmental quality."

> . . . The council has plenty of other ideas for blurring the thin green line between church and state. Claiming that "one of the few areas where jobs are being created is the clean-energy sector" and that "faith- and community-based groups can play a critical role in connecting government green job programs with those that need them most," the report suggests that the administration "encourage the Department of Labor, the Department of Housing and Urban Development and other Federal agencies to work cooperatively with faith-based and neighborhood organizations to ensure that low-income communities and workers with barriers to employment are targeted when creating green job training programs."

One of our trustees, Dr. Edward Blick, professor of science at Oklahoma University for over forty years, and former Air Force weatherman, has written two books exposing global warming and the administration's fight against CO_2 as unfounded vicious lies. We will be pleased to send any pastor a free copy of these books (1-800-652-1144).

If the president's plan to use churches to promote his so-called "green environment program" succeeds, perhaps the 164-page book on the "green gospel" will replace Bibles in the pews.

Paul continued in his letter to the Romans to emphasize the progression of degeneration when a nation begins to believe that there is no Creator and worship the animals instead of God:

> Wherefore God also gave them up to uncleanness through the lusts of their own hearts, to dishonour their own bodies between themselves:

Who changed the truth of God into a lie, and worshipped and served the creature more than the Creator, who is blessed for ever. Amen. For this cause God gave them up unto vile affections: for even their women did change the natural use into that which is against nature: And likewise also the men, leaving the natural use of the woman, burned in their lust one toward another; men with men working that which is unseemly, and receiving in themselves that recompence of their error which was meet. And even as they did not like to retain God in their knowledge, God gave them over to a reprobate mind, to do those things which are not convenient.

—Romans 1:24–28

This pattern of degeneracy occurred in Sodom and Gomorrah, in Greece, and was happening at the time of Paul in Rome, and it is also taking place right now in our schools without any protest from the churches. We read that *by* Jesus Christ and *for* Jesus Christ were all things created. Jesus said, "I am the way, the truth, and the life." When a generation stops worshipping the Creator and starts worshipping the creature, life is turned off and living things begin to die. Our president, by executive order, made June sodomite month; he has appointed many sodomites to high positions in his administration; he has internationally criticized the pastors of Uganda for trying to curb sodomy and protect the children. Paul indicated this would happen if we allowed evolution to be taught in our schools, and he stated that any nation that even condones this degenerative sin is worthy of death. The apostle also warns of the consequences that follow when sodomy infests an entire generation, because that generation is the last one:

For if God spared not the angels that sinned, but cast them down to hell, and delivered them into chains of darkness, to be reserved unto judgment; And spared not the old world, but saved Noah the eighth person, a preacher of righteousness, bringing in the flood upon the world of the ungodly; And turning the cities of Sodom and Gomorrha into ashes condemned them with an overthrow, making them an ensample unto those that after should live ungodly.

—2 Peter 2:4–6

We leave it up to the reader to consider if this is indeed the last generation before Jesus comes.

Sign Number 38

Abortion

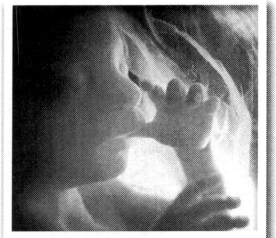

The Supreme Court ruling in the national court case of *Roe v. Wade* made the taking of a life in the womb legal. Since 1971 the abortions per year in the United States that are reported would average approximately 1 million. These are just the reported abortions, as there are doubtless a large number of illegal abortions or late–term abortions that are not reported for obvious reasons. In most states late–term abortions are illegal, and women on the upper rungs of the social ladder want to keep this delicate affair unreported, of course. Also, statistics in the 2010 *World Almanac* (reported through 2005) indicate that California and New Hampshire do not report abortions, and yearly there are usually one or two other states that also do not report the number of abortions performed there. And, of course, we would expect that California with a population of 37 million with its high immigrant ratio and more mixed lifestyles would have close to half a million abortions a year by itself. Along with other non–reporting states, it would be conservative to estimate that since 1971 our yearly abortions in the United States would number 1.5 million, or approximately 60 million total.

One of the arguments for abortion is that there are just too many people in the world and we have to do everything possible to trim it back to 2 billion (some go as low as half a billion). The present population is approximately 7 billion. However, India with a population of 1.1 billion, about a third the size of the United States, has a population density ten times greater than ours.

Growing up on the farm in the 1920s, farmers usually had from five to ten kids to help on the farm to milk the cows, plow the corn, and pick the cotton. As farming implements were developed to plow twenty acres a day, fewer kids were needed and as a larger percentage of our population gathered in urban areas, kids became an expense and a drag. Also, as we have brought out in several of these chapters, with more spare time, leisure, money, cars, and moral decline, in spite of multiple birth control devices and methods, more women were becoming pregnant with unwanted babies. Thus came the way and the means to get rid of them . . . and it is called abortion.

But abortion was not invented by Planned Parenthood. Moses, it seems, about 1500 B.C. had to judge on this matter, and early Christian ecclesiastics were also quite blunt in calling it infant murder, something that only the most biblically based and conservative pastors today have the nerve to condemn. So there be no doubt or controversy as to the early Christian position on this issue, we submit the following from *A Dictionary of Early Christian Beliefs* (published by Hendrickson).

Note: The term "exposing infants" refers to the practice of abandoning infant children along roadsides, leaving them either to die of exposure or to be taken by someone, usually to be raised as a slave or a prostitute.

> You shall not kill the child by obtaining an abortion. Nor, again, shall you destroy him after he is born.
> —Barnabas, c. 70–130

> You shall not murder a child by abortion nor kill one who has been born.
> —Didache, c. 80–140

> They bear children, but they do not destroy their offspring.
> —Letter to Diognetus, c. 125–200

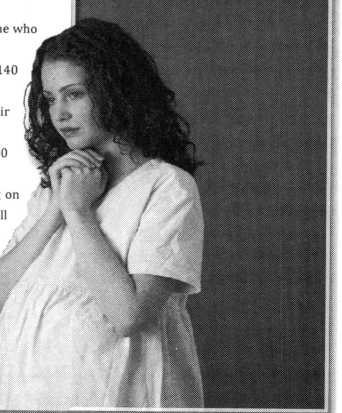

> We say that those women who use drugs to bring on abortion commit murder. And we also say they will have to give an account to God for the abortion. So on what basis could we commit murder? For it does not belong to the same person to regard the very fetus in the womb as a created being (and therefore an object of God's care)—yet, when he has passed into life, to kill him. We also teach that it is wrong to expose an infant. For those who expose them are guilty of child murder.
> —Athenagoras, c. 175

Fathers, forgetting about their children who have been exposed, often unknowingly have intercourse with a son that has debauched himself and with daughters who are prostitutes.

—Clement of Alexandria, c. 195

Although keeping parrots and curlews, the [pagans] do not adopt the orphan child. Rather, they expose children who are born at home. Yet, they take up the young of birds. So they prefer irrational creatures to rational ones!

—Clement of Alexandria, c. 195

What cause is there for the exposure of a child? The man who did not desire to beget children had no right to marry at all. He certainly does not have the right to become the murderer of his children, because of licentious indulgence.

—Clement of Alexandria, c. 195

In our case, murder is once for all forbidden. Therefore, we may not destroy even the fetus in the womb, while as yet the human being derives blood from other parts of the body for its sustenance. To hinder a birth is merely a speedier way to kill a human. It does not matter whether you take away a life that has been born, or destroy one that is not yet born.

—Tertullian, c. 197

First of all, you [pagans] expose your children, so that they may be taken up by any compassionate passer-by, to whom they are quite unknown!

—Tertullian, c. 197

Although you are forbidden by the laws to kill newborn infants, it so happens that no laws are evaded with more impunity or greater safety. And this is done with the deliberate knowledge of the public.

—Tertullian, c. 197

Among surgeons' tools there is a certain instrument that is formed with a nicely-adjusted flexible frame for first of all opening the uterus and then keeping it open. It also has a circular blade, by means of which the limbs within the womb are dissected with careful, but unflinching care. Its last appendage is a blunted or covered hook, by which the entire fetus is extracted by a violent delivery. There is also a copper needle or spike, by which the actual death is brought about in this treacherous robbery of life. From its infanticide function, they give it the name, "killer of the infant"—which infant, of course, had once been alive.

—Tertullian, c. 210

Indeed, the Law of Moses punishes with appropriate penalties the person who causes abortion. For there already exists the beginning stages of a human being. And even at this stage, [the fetus] is already acknowledged with having the condition of life and death, since he is already susceptible to both.

—Tertullian, c. 210

Are you to dissolve the conception by aid of drugs? I believe it is no more lawful to hurt a child in process of birth, than to hurt one who is already born.

—Tertullian, c. 212

I behold a certain ceremony and circumstance of adultery. On the one hand, idolatry precedes it and leads the way. On the other hand, murder follows in company.... Witness the midwives, too! How many adulterous conceptions are slaughtered!

—Tertullian, c. 212

There are some women who, by drinking medical preparations, extinguish the source of the future man in their very bowels. So they commit murder before they bring forth. And these things assuredly come down from the teaching of your gods.

—Mark Minucius Felix, c. 200

Women who were reputed believers began to resort to drugs for producing sterility. They also girded themselves around, so as to expel what was being conceived. For they did not wish to have a child by either a slave or by any common fellow—out of concern for their family and their excessive wealth. See what a great impiety the lawless one has advanced! He teaches adultery and murder at the same time!

—Hippolytus, c. 225

The womb of the wife was hit by a blow of his heel. And, in the miscarriage that soon followed, the offspring was brought forth, the fruit of a father's murder.

—Cyprian, c. 250

I cannot find language to even speak of the infants who were burned to the same Saturn!

—Lactantius, c. 304–313

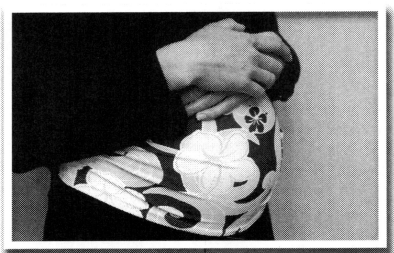

[Speaking of pagans] They either strangle the sons born from themselves, or if they are too "pious," they expose them.

—Lactantius, c. 304–313

Let no one imagine that to strangle new-born children is allowable. For this is the greatest impiety! God breathes into their souls for *life,* not for *death.* Men . . . deprive souls that are still innocent and simple, of the light that they themselves have not given. . . . Or can those persons be considered innocent who expose their own offspring as prey for dogs? As far as their participation is concerned, they have killed them in a more cruel manner than if they had strangled them! . . . Therefore, if anyone is unable to bring up children because of poverty, it is better to abstain from marriage than to mar the work of God with wicked hands.

—Lactantius, c. 304–313

You shall not slay your child by causing abortion, nor kill the baby that is born. For "everything that is shaped and has received a soul from God, if it is slain, shall be avenged, as being unjustly destroyed" [Ezek. 21:23].

—*Apostolic Constitutions,* compiled c. 390

But as to whether abortionists are killing young human beings with eternal souls or just a few ounces of protoplasm, the preceding is superfluous. The real uncontested verdict is, what does God say?

And the children struggled together within her; and she said, If it be so, why am I thus? And she went to enquire of the Lord. And the Lord said unto her, Two nations are in thy womb, and two manner of people shall be separated from thy bowels; and the one people shall be stronger than the other people; and the elder shall serve the younger.

—Genesis 25:22–23

Did not he that made me in the womb make him? and did not one fashion us in the womb?

—Job 31:15

For thou hast possessed my reins: thou hast covered me in my mother's womb. I will praise thee; for I am fearfully and wonderfully made: marvellous are thy works; and that my soul knoweth right well. My substance was not hid from thee, when I was made in secret, and curiously wrought in the lowest parts of the earth.

—Psalm 139:13–15

Thus saith the LORD that made thee, and formed thee from the womb, which will help thee; Fear not, O Jacob, my servant; and thou, Jesurun, whom I have chosen.

—Isaiah 44:2

And, behold, thou shalt conceive in thy womb, and bring forth a son, and shalt call his name JESUS.

—Luke 1:31

We read that God loved Jacob from his mother's womb, and when Jacob and his twin brother Esau were born, Jacob had hold of Esau's heel as a sign that the birthright belonged to him.

Scientific reports are replete with evidence that babies in the womb get hungry, get sleepy, feel pain, and are conscious of their surroundings. It is also indicated according to some reports that they feel the pain during an abortion. I personally have to conclude that abortion is killing an unborn person. I know that some mother who has had an abortion may have extreme guilt after reading this, or some father who has encouraged his wife or girlfriend to have an abortion. Perhaps most who have been involved in an abortion did not understand the seriousness of their act. Maybe they did indeed believe that it was only getting rid of unwanted protoplasm. If so, hopefully they will repent, ask God's forgiveness, and find peace for their souls.

On a larger scale, abortion is a corporate United States crime of murdering 60 million children. This is ten times the number of Jews that Hitler killed in the chambers. If God punished Hitler and Germany for this crime, how much more will He punish or judge us? Unless our nation repents according to 2 Chronicles 7:14, this present generation may be the last.

SIGN NUMBER 39

PUPPET PREACHERS AND MISGUIDED MINISTERS

The Apostle Paul warned us that just before the Antichrist is revealed, there MUST come *apostasia* first (2 Thessalonians 2:3). The King James Version interprets the Greek word *apostasia* as "falling away," indicating a departure from the basic Christian message, which is, salvation by faith in the cross of Christ—a redemptive pardon for all who believe on Him. The Geneva reformers who in 1559 had gone to Switzerland to escape being burned at the stake by the pope, interpreted *apostasia* "departure," evidently going back to 1 Thessalonians 4:13–18 in referring to the departure of the church before the Antichrist is revealed. While this is certainly true, I believe Paul meant a departure from the Gospel of Jesus Christ as delivered to the saints. Jesus said that false christs and false prophets would increase in the last days, and so did Paul and Peter. Jude, a half–brother of Jesus, wrote a brief epistle. I believe his epistle, a prelude to Revelation, was meant especially for the days in which we live. Jude described these so–called "last days preachers" as:

» mockers in the last time

» certain men crept in unawares

» ungodly men, turning the grace of God into greed and lust

» filthy dreamers

» without fear

» spots in your feasts of charity

» trees without fruit
» walking after their own lusts

I am sure we can find today men and women filling the pulpits or speaking on radio or television that have some or all of the preceding qualifications and character- istics referenced by Jude some two thousand years ago.

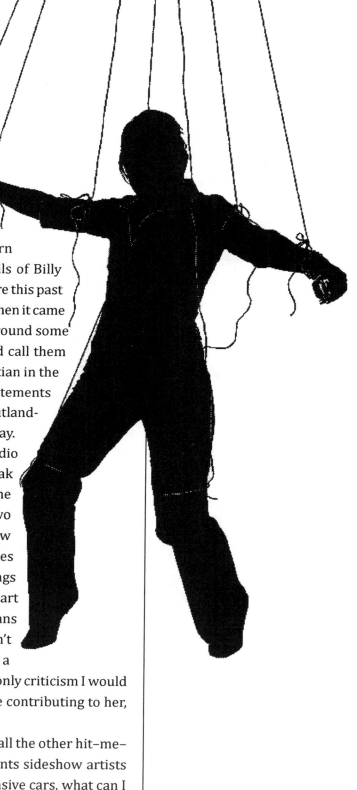

One of the most influential preachers of the last generation who reached many people with the Gospel was Billy Graham. The churches, and especially Southern Baptist churches, had a free ride on the coattails of Billy Graham after 1948 until they got rather threadbare this past decade. Billy Graham, though, had double vision when it came to strict Bible doctrine. He would put his arms around some of the most apostate preachers in the world and call them brothers and laud the pope as the greatest Christian in the world. After Dr. Graham retired, his reported statements concerning Christian faith and service were so outland- ish it is a blessing that God took him out of the way.

There are many good Gospel presenters on radio and television that exalt Jesus Christ and help weak Christians grow in the faith and knowledge of the Lord. Charles Stanley and David Jeremiah are two of these I could mention. I personally do not know what to think of Joel Osteen. To me, he resembles a painted puppet and I keep looking for the strings that move his arms, head, and lips. If there is a part of his message that wins souls or helps Christians to withstand the temptations of the devil, I haven't found it the times I have listened. Joyce Meyers is a tremendously brilliant and talented lady, and the only criticism I would have of her so-called ministry is that millions are contributing to her, thinking they are supporting the Lord's work.

As far as Kenneth Copeland, Benny Hinn, and all the other hit–me– on–the–head or kick–me–in–the–seat–of–the–pants sideshow artists who live in million–dollar homes and drive expensive cars, what can I say that Jude didn't already say?

After Dr. Billy Graham's ministry began to wane in the 1980s, another major ministry began to compete for primary evangelistic

Billy Graham

Joel Osteen

Joyce Meyer

Dr. Rick Warren

stardom, and this was Dr. Rick Warren and his Purpose Driven Church movement, initially financed by the richest man in the world, Rupert Murdoch. Pat Zondervan was a good friend of our ministry, but after Pat went home to be with the Lord, Mr. Murdoch bought Zondervan Publishing, which published and sold 30 million or so copies of *Forty Days of Purpose* by Rick Warren. Dr. Warren then went out to California in one of the most populated but unchurched areas in the United States and mass-mailed a questionnaire, "What Kind of Church Would You Attend?" He established Saddleback Church, a church that non-Christians and secular-minded citizens would attend.

Evidently Dr. Warren sees fundamentalists like me as a roadblock to his becoming the Protestant pope of the world. His associate, Richard Abanes, wrote a book published by the Southern Baptist Sunday School Board attacking me and others as scaremongers. I promptly forced the Southern Baptists at Nashville to remove the book from circulation on the grounds that I was slandered. As I document in my book, *The Dark Side of the Purpose Driven Church,* Dr. Warren has labeled fundamentalists as the most dangerous enemies we have, and the "Five Fundamentals of the Christian Faith" as a narrow and legalistic document. He says he has trained over six hundred thousand pastors, but he doesn't say what he has trained them to do. One thing he has trained them to do, though, is to take over churches. My own former church went from a mission in 1975 to the second largest Baptist Church in Oklahoma in 2004 . . . and then adopted the PDC format. I pass the church every day. Even on Sunday the parking lots are only about one-fourth full, and I understand it is on the verge of bankruptcy. Recently a gentleman from Kansas City laid $52,000 in gold on my desk. He said his church had been the number one evangelical church in Missouri, but it went PDC and it trashed the church. He just wanted to thank me for writing my book. Millions of my tract, "Is Your Church Going Purpose Driven? How Can You Tell?" have gone out, and we at times spend half our days here at the office trying to counsel with church members who have lost their churches to a PDC takeover.

Most pastors today use one of the so-called new versions of the Bible from the Westcott and Hort translation of the Alexandrian texts. In all, in varying degrees, Hell is practically eliminated. Both Mary and Joseph become Jesus' parents, and the unsaved are just being saved when they accept Jesus as Savior. I have also noted that even the word "doctrine" is eliminated or changed to another word that depreciates the meaning.

The Bible by law is forbidden in public schools, and there is no opposition from the church. Our president by executive order makes

June sodomite month and appoints sodomites to high governmental positions, and nothing is said about it from the pulpits. Eighty percent of those in prison come from no-father homes, and nothing is said from the pulpits. The Catholic church spends millions or billions of dollars to pay off court costs and family settlements for priests who have sexually abused children, and little is said about it. Rick Warren told the pastors in Uganda that the choice of being a homosexual was a gift from God, yet this is the only church person in the United States who gets favorable news media notice as America's favorite pastor. The Purpose Driven Church moved the world into the church, and the Emerging Church is moving the church into the world.

When a high school graduate enters a seminary, he is first likely to be told that Moses never wrote the first five books of the Bible and the letters in red were not spoken by Jesus. This is the opening barrage to completely destroy the faith of seminary students; and even if they graduate, they stand in the pulpits believing nothing. Most pastors today in defending themselves against the secular and satanic onslaught give defensive little sermons, and while protecting their 501(c)3 status, are careful not to say anything that will go beyond the steps of their church. They are also careful not to say anything about divorce, adultery, alcohol, sodomy, or gambling lest they offend their membership. Once a week they collect their check and drive to the safety of their church-paid parsonage and few in their immediate area even know they are God's messenger. Their defense is that the church just does not have as much influence in our city or community as it once did. It is no wonder that Jesus asked if He would find faith on earth when He returned.

There are certainly exceptions, but generally this is the picture of the end-time spiritual condition prophesied for the last generation. Are we there yet? Almost!

As I close this chapter, I notice four articles on my desk:

» The Presbyterian Church USA ordains Scott D. Anderson, a homosexual, to the ministry
» Joyce Meyer criticizes Uganda pastors for trying to limit sodomites doing whatever sodomites do
» Conservative Christian groups are getting concerned about Obama's sodomite governmental appointments, but obviously no church group is involved
» MacArthur and Sproul meet with the committee to define the Gospel for churches

When we come to a point in time when most pastors no longer know what the Gospel is, we are certainly in the time of the great falling away. We praise the Lord for those faithful pastors who are still preaching the Word and pointing their memberships to the soon coming of the Lord Jesus Christ.

Sign Number 40

Don't Ignore God

This is the briefest of all the forty signs of the last generation—don't ignore God. We read that the generation before the flood probably lived in a beautiful world, far more abundant and environmentally perfect than the one we now live in. However, they became vicious, self–sufficient, and rebellious. They forgot God, and though Noah preached to them for one hundred and twenty years, they ignored God's warning.

The citizens of Sodom and Gomorrah decided God's way was not what they wanted. Even though righteous Lot doubtless warned them of their evil ways and God even sent angels to give them one last chance, they ignored God's warning. Only three survived the holocaust that followed.

Time and time again Israel would forget the God of their forefathers and be judged severely by droughts, plagues, and foreign invaders. Finally, God sent His only begotten Son to give the nation one last chance, but they not only ignored Jesus their Messiah, they crucified Him. Their cities were burned, more than a million killed, and the rest either sold as slaves or scattered into all the world for two thousand years.

Jesus said that as it was in the days of Noah, and as it was in the days of Lot, so it would be when He came again. The ten sleeping virgins with no oil in their lamps signify the sleeping church today. The

Apostle Peter gave a special warning to the majority of pastors today:

> That ye may be mindful of the words which were spoken before by the holy prophets, and of the commandment of us the apostles of the Lord and Saviour: Knowing this first, that there shall come in the last days scoffers, walking after their own lusts, And saying, Where is the promise of his coming? for since the fathers fell asleep, all things continue as they were from the beginning of the creation. For this they willingly are ignorant of. . . .
>
> —2 Peter 3:2–5

God has given us many signs to let us know that we are living in the last generation. I have listed some forty of these signs, and this last sign is the most significant of all—that in spite of all these signs, only a few are paying attention to what God has said. But this is the way Jesus said it would be. Over and over He said He would come as a thief in the night. His last warning is found in Revelation 16:15: "Behold, I come as a thief. . . ."

One of the most important lessons of the Bible is, **GOD WILL NOT BE IGNORED!!**

Are you ready for the coming of the Lord?